W9-AMX-284

Sailor Moon® the novel #3

Written by
Lianne Sentar

Created by
NAOKO TAKEUCHI

Published by Mixx Entertainment, Inc.
Los Angeles · Tokyo
www.mixxonline.com

RL 4, 008·012

Mixx Entertainment presents
Sailor Moon the novel #3 · *Mercury Rising*
Published on the SMILE Books imprint
ISBN: 1·892213·18·4

Printed in the United States

First printing October 1999

10 9 8 7 6 5 4 3 2 1

Chapter 1
Star Stuck

Beep. Beeeeeep. BEEEEEEP.

"What are you doing? Get out of the way!!"

Serena Tsukino lifted her head up and panicked. The glowing red of the DON'T WALK sign completely freaked her out. She could have sworn it was a green light.

After dodging out of the way to avoid becoming road kill, Serena looked around. Why is everyone looking at me?! she thought. After all, every eighth-grader late for school has to run at the speed of light to avoid being grounded. So, she caused a little traffic accident or commotion every now and then. What was a girl to do?

Glancing at her watch, Serena began to panic.

"Oh, no! I am so late!"

Why did Serena end up having to make this mad dash to school every morning? Not only was it exhausting to run the mile to school, but she had to do it in the A.M. She deserved gym credit for all this unnecessary exercise.

Lately, Serena had been getting way more exercise than she could handle. Ever since Luna, that bossy-little-black talking furball, came into the picture and ruined her life, Serena was going nonstop. It just wasn't fair that her destiny was to become Sailor Moon, Champion of Justice. Beating up sleazy monsters, saving innocent victims, fighting the Enemy—it was exhausting! All Serena really wanted to do was play video games and veg out.

As she ran by, Serena glanced up at a bright poster on a nearby store. She screeched to a halt to check it out. It was an advertisement for the latest pop sensation—SAFFRON LIVE IN CONCERT. Saffron's image smiled down from the poster. She was beautiful, with long, silky blue hair, and

2

sparkling aqua eyes.

Oh God, Serena thought. How could someone who sings bubble-gum music make it so big? Serena was too chic and hip to listen to a plastic teen idol like Saffron. So why did Saffron get all the attention?! These Saffron posters were plastered all over town. Even super-studette heroine Sailor Moon wasn't *that* popular.

Serena rubbed her chin in thought. Maybe she should try marketing herself better. Images of Sailor Moon dolls, Sailor Moon video games, and Sailor Moon movies popped into her head.

"Cool!" Serena exclaimed. "With all that stuff about me, I'd be so popular this novel series would sell like Pokémon cards."

A sudden jerk on one of her ponytails made her screech.

"Ow!" she cried as she grabbed her head. "What was that?"

Her best friend, Molly Baker, ran by at top speed. She hardly stopped to glare at Serena.

"Serena, what are you doing?" Molly yelled, her flaming red hair flowing behind her. "You're gonna be late!"

Serena nearly gagged.

Just her luck, she thought. The best moments for daydreaming were always ruined by that dungeon parents call "school."

"Hold up!" she cried. "Wait, Molly!"

Serena dashed after her friend, and the two jetted as fast as their legs could carry them toward Crossroads Junior High.

Serena stumbled in the door to her homeroom, panting. "Wow!" She heaved. "Molly, the bell didn't ring yet. I can't believe we made it in time."

"And who do you have to thank for that?" Molly put her book bag on her desk and sat down. The class was nearly full of students, though the teacher, Miss Patricia Haruna, hadn't yet shown up.

"Anyway, Serena," Molly said, glancing up. "What were you looking at in that store window? You looked pretty engrossed. You weren't checking out your reflection, were you?"

Serena made a face. Brushing a long ponytail over her shoulder, she sat down in her chair.

4

"It was Saffron," she replied. "Y'know, that new singer? Her poster's plastered all over the place." Serena rested her chin in her palm and sighed. "What's the deal with her, anyway? Personally, I don't think she's worth the hype." Of course, Serena didn't like *any* female singer who took window space from drool-worthy guys like 'NSync.

"She's not bad, but I'm not really into Top 40." Molly fixed the bow in her hair. "It's kinda funny, though. These new singers seem to pop out of nowhere, and in a matter of weeks, they've got all this money and fame. They become stars overnight. Makes you wonder if you could be the next."

The class nerd Melvin suddenly sprang up out of nowhere, his coke-bottle glasses gleaming. "Morning, girls!" he squeaked.

Serena screamed and jumped out of her chair. "Melvin!" she yelled, clenching her fists so hard her knuckles turned white. "You need a bell around your neck to warn people when you're slithering up!"

Melvin adjusted his glasses, a grin plastered

on his round face. "Sorry, but I've got something really cool today," he chirped, whipping out a large, rolled up poster. He unraveled it and held it up. "Check it out!"

It was a poster of Saffron--the same one Serena had seen earlier that day.

"Geez," Serena muttered, sitting back down. "Saffron, Saffron, Saffron. Enough with her already." She shook her head. "If you wanna drool over somebody," she said sneakily, "you should drool over that wicked-cool super-hero Sailor Moon."

"But this girl's got style!" Melvin exclaimed as he pointed to the poster. "The voice, the dancing--people say she's the next Jennifer Lopez! She's all over the Internet."

Serena rolled her eyes. If Melvin had his way, he'd be on the Internet 24-7.

"Melvin!" Molly ordered. "Put that poster away! Miss Haruna will be really mad."

Serena put her head down on her desk. "That's because," she mumbled, "Miss Haruna's jealous of *any* girl that's pretty and thin."

Just then, Serena's classmates Lisa

Brownridge, Kim Matthews, and Rica Kelton walked up. "Hey," Lisa asked, "is that Saffron?"

"She's so beautiful," Kim said with a sigh. "I would kill to have lashes like hers."

Rica brushed a strand of hair behind her ear and leaned against a desk. "Y'know, I heard her agent discovered her in a school just like ours. She's not from any huge show biz family--she's just a normal girl with talent and looks."

"Sounds like me," Serena joked.

Melvin grinned. "She's cool, but I think Serena would make a much better superstar!"

Serena's eyes popped wide open.

"What did you say, Melvin?" Molly asked, surprised.

Melvin held up his index finger as he made his point. "Well, Saffron was just an ordinary girl, right? Serena's glamorous enough to be as big as Saffron is." He turned a shade of red. "And I think...I think Serena's much more beautiful than Saffron!"

The other girls all giggled, but Serena didn't notice. In fact, she was so pleased she forgot to pound Melvin--she always pounded Melvin when he let his crush for her show.

Me, a superstar?

The thought slowly settled into her head. Bright lights, an untouchable wardrobe, boys going nuts, and enough money to play the Sailor V game until she turned old and hobbled--Serena brightened.

What a great idea!

Saffron smiled and accepted the eager girl's notebook. A group of children crowded around the pop star, cheering and squealing happily as Saffron scribbled down her autograph. They clapped as she handed back the signature.

In the darkness of evil shadows, Jedite smiled. His cold eyes focused on Saffron hungrily. "I have a new plan to gather energy, my queen," he whispered.

Queen Beryl waved her long hands over her crystal ball, her sharp nails flashing. "Do tell, Jedite," she drawled.

Jedite smiled. "It seems these foolish humans have made a hero out of this singer Saffron. They hang on her every word, cheer her every move. I believe she is the key to trapping the weak teenagers of this city and draining all their energy."

Queen Beryl's eyes glowed. "Fine, then. Proceed. But you'd best not fail me again, Jedite."

Jedite bowed his head. "Of course, my queen."

Chapter 2
La Vida Loca

After school that day, Molly walked home
with Serena. A cool breeze playfully batted
Serena's golden ponytails.

"So, *what'd* you say we're gonna do again?"
Molly asked as she swung her backpack by her
side.

"Start an act." Serena put an arm around
Molly and grinned. "I've decided to become a star,
Molly, and I need a partner."

Molly cocked an eyebrow. "A star? Serena,
you can't walk and chew gum without falling flat
on your face. You really think you have what it

takes?"

Serena scowled. "I can *too* walk and chew gum. I run at top speed while eating toast every morning."

"True," Molly agreed, rubbing her chin. "I suppose being late every day actually does show-case your many talents."

"You've got to have some drive, Molly," Serena insisted. "Be determined to make it to the top. If Saffron can make it, why can't we?"

Molly looked to the sky. "Well, considering she has the look, the talent, can sing and dance, has charisma..."

"We have all that!"

"Serena, do you remember last year's school play, *The Wizard of Oz*?" Molly narrowed her eyes. "To refresh your memory, the only parts we man-aged to swing were as munchkins. You tripped in the main dancing scene on opening night and knocked a fake tree onto Dorothy."

Serena scowled. Well, so she couldn't sing or dance. And maybe her only real talent was being able to eat a McDonald's Extra Value Meal in four minutes without choking. So what?!

"Stop being so negative, Molly." Serena thrusted her chin in the air. "Just stick with me and you'll be fine."

Molly looked nervous. "Just as long as you don't knock any fake forests down on me."

The two finally arrived at Serena's house. After eating the cookies Serena's mom had left on the table, the two girls ran to Serena's room and dropped their bags on the floor.

Luna, on Serena's bed, awakened from her catnap with a yawn. Serena popped a CD into her stereo, pushed the PLAY button, and Ricky Martin's "Livin' La Vida Loca" blared out of the speakers.

"OK, Molly, follow me!" Serena instructed, striking a pose with her legs shoulder length apart. Molly hesitantly did the same. Then, Serena launched into a crazy dance routine that followed no actual pattern.

"Ready! Two steps left, two steps right, back, forward, kick, twirl!" Serena threw her arms out as she spun around, accidentally whacking Molly in the face.

"Ow!" Molly grabbed her nose. "Serena,

watch where you're--"

"Twirl, kick, forward, back!" Serena did a spin kick like Sailor V, and caught Molly in the chest, knocking the wind out of her.

Molly gasped for breath and doubled over. She shot a furious glance at her friend. "Serena, stop--"

"Back, forward!" This time, Serena stepped on Molly's foot.

Luna watched with wide eyes as Molly hopped around and howled with pain. Serena didn't seem to notice as she danced and twirled, knocking over both lamps and a chair.

"This is great, Molly!" Serena exclaimed as she lept across the room. "We're gonna be stars in no time!"

Just then, the door burst open and Serena's little brother Sammy stomped in, furious.

"Serena!" he yelled, covering his ears. "Turn down your stereo and stop jumping around! You're causing a racket!"

Molly, still holding her foot, turned off the CD. Serena froze in mid-spin, nearly falling over.

"Hey," she complained, looking around the

room. "What happened to the music?"

Sammy crossed his arms and narrowed his eyes. "What are you doing?" he asked flatly. "Mom thought there was an earthquake or something."

"Molly and I are practicing to become super-stars. So buzz off, brat."

Sammy burst into laughter.
"Superstars?" he repeated. "Gimme a break, Serena! The only act you could ever be a part of is a circus act. Though, you'd probably get kicked out within a week for eating all the elephants' peanuts."

Serena narrowed her eyes. Suddenly, her lips curled up into a grin.

"Hey, Sammy," she smirked. "We could use another back-up dancer."

Sammy immediately stopped laughing as Serena advanced slowly on him, eyes glittering wickedly.

"Wh...what?" Sammy sputtered, taking a step backward. "No! I don't wanna be a part of your dumb..."

Serena jumped forward to grab him, and Sammy sped out of the room. He screamed as

Serena chased him down the stairs.

"C'mon, Sammy--you like to dance, right?"

"Mom, tell Serena to leave me alone!"

"We can dress you up, too."

"Eww! Mom, help!"

"You'd look good in a tutu--"

"MOM!!!"

Molly and Luna looked at each other and sighed.

That night, Serena sat on her living room couch with Luna and sulking. The TV was on, but Serena barely noticed.

"Luna," Serena whined as she reached into her popcorn bowl, "it's not fair! Why'd Molly leave so soon this afternoon?"

"She needed medical attention, Serena."

"Cut it out." Serena angrily shoved a handful of popcorn into her mouth. "I don't think she wants to be partners with me," she mumbled.

Luna sighed and rested her head on her paws. "Maybe you and Molly just aren't cut out to be dance partners."

"But we're best friends," Serena moaned.

"We do everything together."

"Bert and Ernie are best friends, but they don't do everything together."

"Are you comparing Molly and me to Muppets?!"

Luna rolled her eyes. "Serena, all I'm saying is that best friends can have differences. If you had everything in common, you'd be so bored you wouldn't be best friends."

Serena pouted and dug her hand back into the popcorn bowl. On TV, *Dawson's Creek* ended. *Funniest Home Videos* was on next, and Serena turned it up.

"At least this'll cheer me up," Serena said, smiling slowly. "For some reason I find people falling down really funny."

Luna cocked an eyebrow. "Because you can relate?"

"Luna!"

A cat appeared on the TV screen, dressed in a tutu. It stood up as its owner waved a fish over its head, then spun around as the owner twirled the fish.

"Look at it go!" the announcer cried. "There

you have it, ladies and gentlemen--a real Catney Spears! See how kitty dances!"

Serena's eyes widened. She jumped up, spilling popcorn all over the floor.

"That's it!" Serena whipped her head at Luna and beamed. "You'll be my partner!"

"*What?*" Luna made a face. "You've got to be kidding."

Serena scooped Luna up in her arms and spun her around. Luna yelped.

"C'mon, Luna!" Serena cried happily as she twirled. "You're a cat that can talk. You must be able to dance, right?" Serena giggled. "People'll love you! Just as long as you don't nag them like you nag me."

Luna frantically tried to jump from Serena's grip, but Serena only held her tighter. "Look," Luna said at last, shaking her paw. "You're Sailor Moon. Stop wasting your time on this stuff--you have to protect the innocent."

Serena frowned. Champion of Justice this, Champion of Justice that, blah, blah, blah. She wanted to be a superstar! She could be a star by day and fight evil by night. Superman had a day job, didn't he?

"Fine," Serena shot as she plopped the cat back down on the couch. "I'll just do a solo act. But don't come to me for an autograph when I become super famous!"

Luna scratched her nose with a paw. "*Infamous* is more like it," she mumbled.

A short girl with coke-bottle glasses nervously pulled on her dress as she stood outside Molly's doorway. She rang the doorbell again, then whipped her head around to make sure no one was watching.

Molly opened the door at last. The short girl rushed in.

"Melvin, you're here!"

"Shhhhh!" Melvin pressed a finger to his lips and squirmed in his dress. "Quiet, Molly! If anyone sees me dressed like this, I'll be branded a dork for the rest of my life!"

"Well, it might be a little too late for that." Molly giggled as she closed the door behind him.

Melvin pouted. "Why do I have to wear this anyway, Molly? Why can't I--"

"The dance routine I have planned is for two girls," Molly answered. "Since dancing with Serena will probably get me killed, you're gonna be my partner."

Melvin adjusted his glasses. "Molly, I think it's great you wanna be a star and you wanna let me be your partner, but..." His voice trailed off as he looked down at his dress. "I just really don't think this is my color. Don't you think I'd look better in something mauve, or maybe lavender?"

"You look very pretty, Melvin." Molly giggled as she put an arm around his shoulder. "Now, let's go over our act. We're gonna be superstars, just wait and see!"

Saffron stepped through her apartment door and sighed. The pop star shook out her long, blue hair and threw her car keys onto the kitchen table.

"What a day!" Saffron exhaled as she sat down and pulled off her stylish pumps. "Signing autographs is exhausting. Fun, but exhausting."

Suddenly, there was a CRASH from the next room. Saffron jumped up.

"What was that?" she cried as she ran

toward the sound. When she got to the bedroom door, she froze.

Standing by the shattered window was a witch—a hideous witch. More than seven feet tall, with red hair and blue skin, the witch turned shining yellow eyes at the singer.

"Hello, little one," the witch drawled with a grin.

Saffron gasped, then spun around and bolted. "Help!" she screamed as she ran toward her front door. "Somebody, please--"

Something freezing burned around Saffron's leg, causing her to trip and fall. Her leg was half-covered in ice.

"What?" she cried, eyes wide.

The witch slowly walked toward her, a cruel grin on her lips. "I'm afraid you can't escape, Miss Fame. Don't worry, my ice will take good care of you."

With that, the witch thrust out her hands and shot a stream of thick blue ice at the floored star. Saffron screamed as the ice coated her, but her cries were cut off as the ice completely encased her body. The witch laughed as the frozen Saffron stared out from the chunk of ice, her mouth still open in a silent scream.

"Easy enough," the witch commented as she looked down at herself. "Now for the fun part."

The witch closed her fist, and blue light flashed from her body. When the light cleared, she stood as an exact copy of Saffron, right down to the outfit.

The witch pulled a compact from Saffron's purse and examined her reflection in the mirror. "Excellent. I look just like her." Her fangs flashed in the glass.

"And now for Jedite's plan." She chortled an evil laugh. "The humans of this city don't stand a chance."

Chapter 3
Star Quest

"Left and right and back and KICK and right and left and forward and KICK and--"

"Serena!" Luna yelled, covering her ears with her paws. "Turn the music down! Please!"

"I can't hear you, Luna." Serena hummed as she spun. "Don't you know to never distract an artist when she's in the moment?"

Luna jumped at the radio and flipped the dial. The blaring "Baby One More Time" that Serena had been dancing to was replaced with quiet Mozart.

Serena whipped her head at the cat. "Luna,

why'd you change the station?" she shouted. "I was finally getting the pattern down!"

"If your 'pattern' was to shake the house and shatter my favorite glass, then you've already succeeded." Luna grumbled as she rested her head on her paws. "And I'm worried about your safety. Music that loud is terrible for your ears. Do you want to lose your hearing?"

"Huh?" Serena cupped her hand around her ear. "Say that again, Luna, I couldn't hear you."

Luna sighed.

Just then, the music on the radio ended, and a commercial drifted out of the speakers.

"Hey, everyone," the voice of Saffron exclaimed. "Do you want to make it to the lights and fame of stardom?"

Serena snapped to attention.

"For all the teenagers out there who dream of making it big," Saffron cooed, "here's your chance! Come to *Star Quest* outside Crossroads Mall and show me your talent. First place winners get a record deal, and an instant ticket to success!"

Serena's jaw dropped. Here it was, her chance! This was exactly what she'd been waiting the most for! Well, she'd been waiting for the *Sailor V* movie to come out more than anything, but this was a close second.

"Did you hear that, Luna?" Serena cried, jumping into the air. "A contest! Winner becomes a star! Oh, I am so fit to win!"

Luna got up and jumped onto Serena's desk. "Serena," the cat warned. "Don't rush into anything. I mean, isn't this contest a little fishy, popping out of nowhere? Saffron's a big star, shouldn't there have been press about this weeks before the actual contest? And why advertise on a classical station? That makes no sense."

Serena stuck her tongue out as she changed out of her sweat suit and into her CK jeans and t-shirt. "You're suspicious of everything fun, Luna. I swear, next thing you're going to be telling me is that body glitter was set up by the bad guys to suck up teenagers' energy."

"Speaking of which," she said as she squeezed body glitter from a bottle and spread it around her eyes. She threw her favorite Delia's hair clips in her hair and picked up her purse.

"Wait," Luna called as she jumped after the

girl. "Serena, listen to me. If you keep being so careless, the Enemy might succeed in taking over--"

But Serena was already jumping down the staircase. Luna shook her head and ran after her.

"Why do I bother?" she muttered as she chased her Champion of Justice out the door.

There was a huge crowd in front of Crossroads Mall. Teenagers from all over the city had come to compete in Saffron's *Star Quest*.

"Oh my God," Serena murmured, covering her mouth. "Luna, look how many people showed up."

"Good," Luna said quickly. "Now that you see it's nearly impossible to win, you can forget about performing and investigate."

Serena looked at her in disbelief. "Are you kidding?" Serena laughed, slapping her fist into her palm. "This is my audience! Now I'll be able to show how talented I am in front of all these people!"

The crowd suddenly hushed. A stage had been set up in front of the mall, and a young, blond man in a pair of Ray Ban sunglasses and a Nike cap walked onto the stage.

"Hello, everybody!" he cried in a voice that sounded oddly familiar. "Are you ready to strut your stuff?"

The crowd cheered. Serena squinted at the man. There was something about him, besides the fact that he was a hottie. He looked familiar, kind of like that stupid guy from the radio station, Jedite. Could Luna be right about the Enemy being behind the contest?

Serena shook her head. She was becoming as paranoid as Luna. The *last* thing she wanted was to suspect that everything cool was an Enemy plot.

"Serena," the cat whispered from her feet. "Doesn't that announcer look like Jed--"

"Shh," Serena hushed. "I'm trying to listen, Luna."

"Here are the rules," the blond man announced. "Try-outs begin today. Everyone needs a partner for their act, and you'll perform after sign-up is completed. At the end of the day, Saffron herself will announce who makes the final round."

Everyone cheered and rushed to the sign-up tables in front of the stage. Serena picked up Luna.

"Did you hear that?" Serena exclaimed. "Two to an act. Oh, Luna, you have to be my partner!"

Luna's face turned red with anger. Serena winced. Uh-oh, she thought. She knew that look—she was going to get it.

"Serena!" Luna exploded. "You haven't listened to a word I've said. I told you--you have no time for this! You're Sailor Moon, defender of the innocent, and you have to keep your mind and body focused on that!"

Serena pouted. "But this is my dream!"

"Some dreams have to be put on hold for the sake of the innocent, Serena." Luna shook her head. "You've been ignoring too much. This contest appeared out of nowhere. Plus, the announcer looks and sounds like Jedite--this must be an Enemy plot! You have to investigate!"

Serena's lip trembled. "But...I wanted to be rich and famous!"

Serena began to wail. "No fair!" she cried as

tears gushed down her cheeks. "I want to have my posters all over the city for boys to drool over. I want to dress up in stylin' clothes and go on stage. I want to be rich!"

Serena shoved Luna to the ground and ran off crying. Luna stared in disbelief, then chased after her.

"Serena!"

Serena ran into a small side alley and leaned against the brick wall. She buried her face in her hands as she cried.

She wanted to be a star. Now, that would never happen, she thought. And here she was, crying in some little alley without a friend in the world.

Well, Serena hadn't actually lost any of her friends or anything, but it still felt like she was alone!

She sniffed and started crying harder. She wasn't really that sad, just disappointed, and a good wail always made her feel better.

"Hiding from something, blondie?"

Serena froze. Her tears immediately

stopped as she slowly looked up.

Serena turned bright pink as her eyes met two dark blue ones. The dark-haired guy who always loved to tease her was looking down at her, one eyebrow cocked.

Oh my God, Serena thought as she quickly turned her face. Did that jerk see me cry?

"What do *you* want?" Serena snapped as she furiously tried to brush away her tears.

The young man shrugged as he leaned against the wall. "Here for *Star Quest*?" he asked.

Serena was suddenly struck by an idea. An imaginary light bulb went on over her head.

She needed a partner, she thought as she glanced up at him. Maybe this creep would do an act with her.

But Serena realized that was a bad idea. She could see it now--*Ladies and Gentlemen, I present to you two people who can argue without breathing for a half-hour straight!*

"I was going to try out," Serena sighed, "but it interfered with some of my responsibilities."

He smirked. "Aw, I wanted to see your per-formance. What were you planning to do? Down a few pizzas, a bag of donuts, and an entire cake in record time?"

"Get lost!" Serena hissed. "I'm having a bad day." She was so frustrated and upset that she couldn't even think of a clever comeback.

"Bad day, huh? I pity your family." He walked away, calling behind him, "Just don't eat to drown your anger, you certainly don't need the extra calories!"

Serena practically felt steam come out of her ears. *Jerk!* He was always so mean to her! Making fun of her hobbies, her eating habits, her hair.

But despite her anger, she felt her heart beating a little crazily in her chest. And she couldn't stop thinking about how his eyes seemed the exact color of the ocean, glistening and rippling under the sun on a bright summer day.

The next morning, Serena burst through the front doors of Crossroads Junior High just as the last bell rang.

"No!" she shouted as she dashed up the stairs. "No, I can't be late again!" She reached her homeroom door and dashed into the classroom.

mercury rising

"I'm here," she called as she ran to her desk. "Miss Haruna, I'm here."

Miss Haruna looked up from her attendance sheet, eyeing Serena. "You're lucky today, Serena," she murmured as she made a check in her book. "I was just getting to your name."

Serena grinned. *All right! No detention!*

Serena looked around. Her classmates were decorating the room with brightly colored balloons and streamers. Everyone was chatting excitedly.

"Hey, Serena." Molly walked up, her eyes bright. "Isn't this exciting?"

"Yeah." Serena agreed. "Really exciting. I mean, I thought I was gonna be late, but I guess I was running faster than I--"

"I didn't mean you getting in on time," Molly said sourly. "I meant the decorations. The whole class is preparing for *Star Quest*. We all made tonight's final round."

Serena wilted. "Oh." She rested her head on her arms and scowled. "Is that all?"

Molly patted Serena on the head. "C'mon, Serena, don't be upset. You can come watch."

Serena frowned. Yeah, like *that* would make

her feel better. Watch someone else become the star she wanted to be.

But then Serena remembered what Luna had said about investigating. She didn't want Luna nagging her about not being a responsible super-hero, so she figured she'd follow the bossy cat's advice before she got yelled at.

"It *might* be interesting. Maybe I'll show," Serena said at last. Maybe they'll be selling cotton candy, she added to herself.

Molly giggled and leaned forward to whisper in Serena's ear. "Melvin's my dance partner. Wait'll you see him in his dress!"

Serena's eyes nearly popped out of her head. "A DRESS?!"

Molly nodded, giggling harder.

Serena started to laugh. Melvin, in a dress? Now she'd definitely go, even if Luna had never suggested it!

Serena took the bus to the Crossroads Theater that night. Luna rode along on her shoulder.

"Wow." She whistled as she looked at the

lights strung around the building. "This show's gonna be big."

"Just remember, Serena--keep your eyes peeled for any sign of the Enemy." Luna flicked her head around, alert.

"Yeah, yeah, whatever," Serena answered flatly. "Don't hurt your eyes looking for a monster to pop out of the ceiling." She walked into the auditorium and strolled down the aisle. She was the only one there.

"Hey, this is weird," she commented as she checked her watch. "The performance is supposed to be starting now. Where is everyone?"

Luna narrowed her eyes. "I don't like this, Serena. Check backstage."

"Fine." Serena stepped up onto the stage and pulled aside the curtain. She froze.

Saffron was standing with her back to Serena, holding up a small brooch. The pin was sucking the energy out of hundreds of costumed teenagers lying unconscious on the floor.

"Molly!" Serena gasped as she saw her friend on the floor. "Melvin, Lisa, everyone!" Serena reached out and grabbed Saffron by the shoulder. "What are you doing to them?"

The pop star slowly turned her head. Serena jumped back when she saw the face. It was not the face of Saffron, but the face of a witch with blue skin and yellow eyes.

"Oh," the witch murmured. "Looks like I missed one." She turned around and pointed her weird brooch at Serena.

The witch's fangs flashed. "Ready to join your pals, little girl?"

Chapter 4
Smile! You're on Candid Camera!

Serena covered her mouth in horror.

"Something wrong, dear?" The witch aimed her brooch at Serena's forehead.

"Eeewwwww!!!!!" Serena screamed, disgusted. "Ew, Saffron! You've gotten so ugly! What did you do? Use a bad brand of make-up or something? You look like a monster!"

The witch dropped her aim momentarily, confused by Serena's reaction.

"That is a monster!" Luna hissed into Serena's ear. "That's one of the Enemy, disguised as Saffron!"

"Oh!" Serena laughed at herself. "That makes more sense. Boy, for a second there I was afraid my Cover Girl make-up was gonna make me look like you!"

The witch snarled. "Now you've angered me. Prepare to surrender your energy to the Negaverse!"

Serena got the hint. She jumped off the stage, and ran through the doors to the lobby.

"Geez, Luna." Serena panted as she dashed into the women's bathroom and slammed the door shut behind her. "How come you've always gotta be right?"

"That witch is trying to absorb energy from all the contestants," Luna said quickly, jumping from Serena's shoulder. "You must defeat her to save your friends."

Serena nodded, sucking in deep breaths. "Right. Time for some fireworks!" She thrust her hand into the air.

"MOON PRISM POWER MAKE-UP!"

The bathroom filled with lights that flashed with crazy tie-die colors. When the light show ended, Serena was Sailor Moon.

mercury rising

"OK," Serena declared, brushing a strand of loose hair from her face. "What do you think, Luna? Should I sneak up on her from behind, or from the side?"

The bathroom door crashed open, and the fuming witch stood in the doorway.

Serena's eyes widened. "Or she could find me and I could run away screaming. I kinda like that plan."

"Be strong, Sailor Moon!" Luna cried. "Use your tiara!"

"Oh, no!" the witch shouted. "I've heard of you. You're that bratty Sailor girl. Prepare to die!" The witch raised her hands and shot a stream of thick ice directly at Serena.

Serena yelped and jumped out of the way. The ice bolt hit a sink, freezing it over immediately.

"She shoots *ice?!*" Serena panicked. "Oh, man, if I'm not careful, I'm gonna become a giant Slurpee!"

The witch roared and fired again. Serena ducked into a stall.

"Sailor Moon!" Luna cried. "Get out, she'll have you trapped!"

Too late. The witch stepped into the stall's doorway, blocking Serena's escape.

"One Sailor brat on ice, coming up!" the monster-formerly-known-as-Saffron roared. She raised her hands and fired.

Serena dove out of the way. The ice stream shattered against the wall as Serena slid between the witch's legs. Serena jumped up and pushed the witch full force into the stall.

"One evil witch in the toilet, coming up!"

The witch toppled headfirst into the toilet bowl. Serena ran to the toilet and flushed it, then dashed out of the bathroom.

Serena laughed as she headed for the auditorium. "That was great, Luna! Why can't I have this much fun fighting all the time?"

"Quickly!" Luna ordered. "She'll be after us in a second."

Serena dashed into the auditorium and pulled down the huge light switch--the auditorium went dark. Serena ran to the stage.

The witch appeared in the dark doorway a moment later, dripping wet. "You little brat!" she screamed as she stumbled into the dark theater.

mercury rising

"Where are you? I'll suck your energy dry!"

"All teenagers dream of being superstars." Serena's voice echoed commandingly through the theater. "You have toyed with this dream, and for that you must pay. Lights, Luna!"

Luna, above the stage, pulled a lever. A single, bright spotlight fell on Sailor Moon. There she stood, arms crossed and eyes glittering.

Serena grinned. Wow, she thought, this had to be her best entrance ever. What stage presence! Her school had been crazy to cast her as a munchkin—she could have played the Wizard of Oz himself.

"Sailor Moon!"

Luna's voice jolted Serena out of her daydreaming. She shook her head and got back to making her threatening speech.

"Evil will never have its way as long as I'm here!" she shouted. "I am Sailor Moon, Champion of Justice and defender of young people's dreams, and on behalf of the moon, you're punished!"

The witch snarled. "Shut up!" she spat as she launched a huge wave of ice.

"Aaawww!" The Champion of Justice and

defender of young people's dreams screamed as she dove off the stage into a row of chairs.

"That ice beam's much stronger than before." Serena panted as she hid beneath the seats. "What am I gonna do? Maybe she won't find me here..."

"Aha!"

"Then again, maybe she will." Serena sucked in a breath and jumped up. She ran down the aisle.

"Not so fast!" the witch shouted.

Something cold engulfed Serena's legs. She collapsed, screaming. The witch cackled as the superhero desperately tried to move her frozen legs.

"It's no use, Sailor brat." The witch sneered as she held up her palms. "Nothing can break free of my ice. Say your prayers."

Serena covered her face with her arms as the witch shot another wave of ice, but it was no use. Serena's body froze over quickly.

"Lu...na..." Serena choked as her body became completely trapped in a giant ice cube.

The witch laughed maniacally. "I've done it!" she declared. "I've defeated her! This city will

mercury rising

be the Negaverse's for eternity!"

Just then, something red streaked through the air and landed in the ice with a chunk. A red rose.

The witch stared at it. "Huh?"

A long crack traveled down from the razor sharp stem. The ice shattered--Serena fell to the floor, gasping.

"No!" The witch turned furious yellow eyes toward the balcony. "Who threw that?"

"There are those who dream," Tuxedo Mask said quietly, arms crossed over his chest, "and there are those who protect those who dream." He tipped his hat up, and smiled coldly at the witch. "And I protect the protector."

"Tuxedo Mask!" Serena panted happily.

He focused his eyes on her. His gaze made her melt into nothingness. Oh, how she wished he didn't have that mask to cover his eyes! *Who was he?*

"Sailor Moon," Tuxedo Mask whispered. "Believe in yourself. Your friends are in danger, and you're the only one who can save them. Don't let this refrigerator ice maker attack the innocent

41

dreamers of the city."

"Refrigerator ice maker?" the witch shrieked. "How dare you call me that, top hat boy!" She aimed her palms at him and prepared to fire.

"I've had enough of you!" Serena shouted, getting to her feet. "You attack my friends, you freeze me over, and you try to ice my dream guy? Prepare to get dusted, creepette!" She ripped off her tiara and threw it as hard as she could.

"MOON TIARA ACTION!"

"NO!!" the witch screamed, but it was no use. In a second she was vaporized, her energy-sucking brooch lying on top of the pile of dust.

Serena walked over to the brooch and crushed it under her boot. "Sayonara, you cheap piece of jewelry."

Blue light seeped from the broken pin, and the unconscious teenagers slowly began to stir. Luna jumped down from the stage and ran to Serena.

"Good work, Sailor Moon," said Luna. "The kids are safe, and I'm sure the real Saffron will be all right now, too."

Serena smiled, then looked up at the balcony sadly. "Tuxedo Mask's gone." She sighed. "I was hoping to talk to him after the fight."

"Talk to him about what?"

Serena turned red. "I don't know. Maybe ask him if he'd catch a soda with me. He's such a babe."

"Be careful, Sailor Moon," Luna said. "You know nothing about him--"

But Serena was already lost in thought, giggling about how she would one day win over Tuxedo Mask.

Luna shook her head. "Just my luck," she muttered, "that my destined defender of the world has to be so boy crazy."

Serena sucked on the straw of her Baskin Robbins Smoothie and kicked her shoes off.

"Ah!" She sighed as she collapsed happily on her bed. "Another night, another villain foiled. We should get ice cream after every battle, Luna."

Luna jumped up on the bed and curled by Serena's side. "You deserve a treat for being so good about all this," the cat replied. "I know you really wanted to be in that contest, but you gave it up and fought on a school night for the sake of the world."

Serena giggled. "If it keeps me from doing my homework, I'll do anything, Luna."

"That's right! You have a math test tomorrow!"

"Oh, but I'm so tired from that battle," Serena complained loudly as she hugged her pillow and closed her eyes. "Too bad, I'll study in class."

"Please, Serena, you can't fail another--"

"Good night, Luna. Sweet dreams."

Serena pulled her pillow over her head and smiled. She knew just who she was going to dream about. Maybe this Champion of Justice stuff wasn't so bad after all.

Serena drifted off to sleep that night with a grin on her face, seeing nothing in her mind but Tuxedo Mask's smile.

Chapter 5
Who Is That Girl,
And Who
Does Her Hair?

It was a Wednesday night, and Serena was enjoying being seriously lazy. She lounged on her comfy couch, her best pair of Old Navy loafing socks on, her Backstreet Boys' *Millennium* CD in the stereo, and a bag of Doritos open by her side. She propped her *SMILE* magazine in her lap and laughed.

"Oh, Kemmy, you are so rockin'!" She giggled as she swung her feet. "I wish I could be a sushi delivery girl!"

Every once in a while she could steal a bite, she added to herself. Wow. Sushi all the time?

Talk about heaven.

"Serena?" her mother called from the other room. "Is that you, dear?"

"Yeah, Mom," Serena answered as she popped another Dorito in her mouth. "Do we have any Snapple left? I'm getting majorly thirsty from these chips."

Mrs. Tsukino walked into the doorway, a baking spoon still in her hand. "Well, I see you're all fit for a night in," she said, lowering her eyelids. "And how did that test today go, Miss Comic Books?"

"I dunno, test results come in tomorrow."

Mrs. Tsukino slapped her spoon against her palm. "You know that if you don't do well on this one," she said lowly, "you're going to be in some serious trouble, Missy."

Serena winced. Her mom was always so rough on her because of her grades. Serena was Champion of Justice, how could she find time for studying between all her relaxing? Besides, it wasn't *that* big a deal to be bad at tests. And quizzes. And homework. And school in general.

"But I had a complete blank-out when I got

it," she complained. "I can't promise good results." She decided not to add that the blank-out was a result of not studying at all, and that it wasn't really a blank-out, it was just her not knowing any of the answers.

"Serena," her mother sighed. "It's always the same old thing with you. With your grades, I find it hard to believe you're trying at all."

"Oh, I try," Serena answered. "A little. But Mom, school's so hard, and video games are so much more fun."

Her mother plucked the magazine out of her hand. "Upstairs with you," she ordered, pointing her spoon like a general's sword. "I want you to study for the next hour, then go to sleep."

"But Mom!" Serena complained. "It's Wednesday! Wednesday is potato chip and comic book day. I can't just break a tradition at a snap of the fingers."

"Well, then, will you study tomorrow?"

Serena frowned. "But Thursday is video game and milkshake day."

"Friday?"

"Movie night."

"Saturday?"

"Shopping with the girls."

"Sunday?"

"Listening to music and talking on the phone."

Mrs. Tsukino crossed her arms. "And what about Monday and Tuesday?"

"Those are veg nights in front of the TV." Serena smiled. She was proud of her schedule--it planned a wide variety of activities for her, and best of all, none of those activities involved home-work.

"Enough excuses," her Mom snapped, waving her spoon at Serena's nose menacingly. "Upstairs. Now."

Serena sighed as she turned towards the stairs. Her mother reached out and snatched the bag of chips.

"Hey!" Serena cried. "Mom, study is torture enough, but at least let me pig out!"

"Your diet is horrendous. You have to start eating right." Her mother gave Serena a nudge towards the staircase. "Go."

Serena moaned as she clomped up the stairs

to her room. How could her mother do this to her?
It was child abuse! Deprived of food, locked away,
and threatened with a utensil--the child welfare
people would have a field day with this!

Serena opened her door, stepped over the
clothes strewn on the floor, and collapsed onto her
bed. "How can I possible study?" She groaned. "I
already had to deal with one test today. This over-
load'll turn my brain to tapioca."

"Serena?" Luna looked up from her resting
position on the desk. She jumped over to sit beside
the girl.

"What's the matter?" the talking feline
asked. "You look like someone just told you
Bovinity Dovinity ice cream was going to be taken
off of Ben and Jerry's flavors list."

"Mom's forcing me to study," Serena muttered. "Can you believe her?"

Luna brightened. "That's great. A little
brain work will do you good. You need to get
away from those awful comic books."

"Awful? Luna, you traitor!" Serena hissed.

"Speaking of brain work, my lazy Champion
of Justice," Luna said, touching her chin with a

paw. "I've been doing a lot of research to find the Moon Princess lately. Anytime you wanna jump in and help," she added sarcastically, "feel free."

Serena shook her head and sighed. "No way, Luna," she mumbled. "Dealing with school and Mom and monsters is enough for me as it is."

"Thought so," Luna muttered. "You know, Serena, once we do find this princess, you have to protect her. It's not like we're going to be dumping her off on the next rocket to the moon."

"In that case, I hope she's cooler than the cat that was sent to find her." Serena sighed and scratched her cheek. Moon princesses, witches, demons, hottie blond villains--this super-hero stuff was weird.

Then again, Serena thought, she wasn't exactly complaining about the hottie blond villains.

The moon was a sliver of pearly light in the sky, dancing in and out of passing clouds. As the shadows crawled across the city, a small black cat slipped through the street and into the back door of the Crown Arcade.

Luna scanned the rows of video games in

the darkened arcade. She found the Sailor V machine, and hopped onto it. She pressed the ON button.

"Welcome to Sailor V." The game buzzed. "Please insert a quarter and help Sailor V trash villains and save the day."

"This is Luna," Luna whispered into the machine's speakers. "Code name 0091. Password is 'Sailor V rocks the house.'"

The video game made an odd beeping noise, then asked: "Why does Sailor V rock the house?"

"Because she bashes the bad guys and amazes the world with her beauty." Luna rolled her eyes at the lame password.

The game unit made another beep. "Welcome, Luna," it said at last. "What new information have you found regarding the moon princess?"

"Not much," Luna said with a sigh. "You're the secret communicating system of the moon, why don't you tell me?"

A picture popped up on the game screen. It was of a teenage girl, Serena's age and with short, blue hair and dark blue eyes.

"This girl's name is Amy Anderson." The game buzzed. "She just transferred to Serena's school. There is a strong presence about her, she is suspected of working for the Enemy."

"All right." Luna nodded. "I'll check up on her right away."

Serena's eyes were wide. She couldn't look away from the test scores posted on the wall. She was too frozen in horror.

"I got LAST?!" Serena choked, gripping her ponytails in both her hands. "Oh my God! A 17! Mom's gonna have my hide!"

Serena collapsed to the tiled floor.

"Don't feel too bad, Serena," Molly said, as Serena rocked on the floor and moaned. "I mean, I did poorly, too. I got an 84. I never get 84's."

"Thanks for making me feel better, Molly!" Serena shouted angrily as she covered her face with her hands. Oh, man, she thought. She knew someone had to finish last, but why was it always her?

"But Serena," Molly said, "check out who got

the highest score--it was that new girl, Amy. She not only got the best grade in our school, she got the highest score in Japan."

Serena looked up. "Really? I didn't know our school had someone that smart." Serena had always thought Melvin was the smartest, but he had never been ranked number one in the country.

"Yeah, we have the real extremes," Molly said with a smirk. "I mean, we have the super-brain Amy, and then we have...you."

Serena scowled. "And then we have the good, stick-with-you-through-everything friends, and then we have...you."

Molly crossed her arms behind her head. "Amy's a little hard to believe, though. A wicked brain child. They say her IQ's 300."

Serena's eyes widened. 300?! She couldn't read that many pages of a book. She couldn't picture someone that smart. With that many brain cells, Serena thought, wouldn't you have a head the size of a watermelon? Boy, that'd look pretty weird.

"I heard she goes to that new Crystal Seminar Cram School," Serena said. "You have to be a genius to go there."

"Did somebody ask for a genius?" Melvin asked as he suddenly popped out of nowhere. Serena jumped in surprise, then scowled at him.

"Melvin!" Serena growled. "We were talking about smart people, not dorks."

Rica looked over from checking her score. "Hey," she said. "You guys talking about Amy?"

"Yeah," Molly answered. "She goes to that expensive brain school for free because she's so smart. If that's not genius material, I don't know what is."

"Look," Melvin exclaimed, pointing towards the window. "There she is right there."

Serena turned around. A thin girl was sitting on the large windowsill and looking down at the courtyard. Her blue hair was cropped stylishly short, and her navy eyes focused quietly on the outdoors.

"I heard she's a real snob," Rica whispered. "You know how the brainy kids are--they think they're better than everyone else."

Molly and Melvin nodded in agreement, but Serena couldn't stop staring at the girl's sad expression. She looks kind of lonely, Serena thought to herself.

"But what a great haircut she's got," Molly said. She tugged on one of Serena's ponytails. "Maybe you should cut your hair short like that, Serena."

"What?!" Serena immediately forgot all about the girl and whipped around to her best friend. "Are you kidding?!" she cried as she pulled her ponytail away. "It took me fourteen years to grow my hair this long! It's my pride and joy, and I'll never cut it!"

Rica laughed. "I've never seen hair as long as yours, Serena. Pantium Pro-V would hire you for commercials in a second." She cocked an eyebrow. "Though considering what a klutz you are, I'm surprised you don't trip over it."

Serena shrieked in anger. Molly and Melvin laughed and made more jokes about Serena's hair. The four friends forgot about the quiet, blue-eyed girl.

Amy slowly glanced over. She took a long look at the laughing students, then turned away and sadly closed her eyes.

Chapter 6
Sailor V to
the Extreme

Serena walked home by herself after school.

Her mom was going to skin her for that test grade, she thought miserably. She considered running away for a few days. Then, when she finally turned up, her mom would be so happy to see her she'd forget all about the test.

Serena moaned. "That won't work!" she cried aloud. "I tried it before, but Mom figured out I was hiding at the arcade and dragged me home after a few hours."

Serena pursed her lips and tried to think of another escape plan, when she saw someone walking up the next block.

"Hey. It's that brain-girl, Amy. She walks home this way?"

Amy didn't carry a backpack like everyone else--she carried an old-fashioned book bag with iron clasps, like in those old Oliver Twist-type movies. She held the bag in front of her thighs as she walked, and didn't look up from the ground.

She really does look lonely, Serena thought sadly.

Just then, Luna jumped out of a tree and onto Amy's shoulders. Amy cried out in surprise, then saw that it was only a cat. She let out a sigh of relief.

"Goodness," Amy said. "You scared me. What are you doing here, kitty?"

Serena's eyes widened. *What is Luna doing here? And jumping on perfect strangers like that? Did that tuna she ate yesterday go bad or something?*

But Luna appeared to be looking over Amy closely. Amy smiled again and scratched Luna's chin.

"My, you're pretty," Amy said. Her voice was high and delicate, but kind. "Do you have an owner? I wish I had a cat like you, but my apartment doesn't allow pets."

Luna slowly stopped analyzing Amy, and purred as the girl petted her head. Serena couldn't believe it. Luna was never that mild-tempered and cute. It looked like the school genius had a way with animals.

"That crescent moon." Amy examined Luna's forehead. "It looks like birthmark. Or is your owner a mean little boy who shaved it there?"

Serena's eyes turned red. She was not a mean little boy! She would inform this genius that Luna's owner was an attractive and popular teen chick. Serena stomped forward and practically yanked Luna off of Amy.

"Excuse me," she muttered, putting Luna on her own shoulder. "This is my cat. Sorry she jumped on you--she's kind of a brat."

Amy laughed and waved a hand. "Oh, that's OK. I think your kitten's sweet." She cocked her head to one side. "What's his name?"

Serena stifled a giggle as Luna meowed indignantly beside her ear. "She's a girl," Serena answered. "Her name's Luna."

Amy blushed. "Oh," she mumbled as she reached over and patted Luna's head. "I'm sorry, Luna."

Serena watched Amy's slim hand stroke the cat, and suddenly got an idea. Amy's a genius, she thought, probably the smartest girl in school. If they became friends...

Serena started to giggle. If they became friends, maybe Amy would tell her the answers to the tests—then she'd ace them all and her mom wouldn't yell at her anymore.

"Are you OK?" Amy asked.

Serena suddenly realized she was giggling like a madwoman. She stopped abruptly and coughed.

"Ahem. Yeah. I'm fine." Serena stuck out a hand and smiled. At the very least, Amy had so many brain cells, a few were sure to rub off on Serena.

"I'm Serena Tsukino," Serena declared. "Nice to meet you."

Amy stared at Serena's hand a moment, then finally put her own slim one in Serena's and shook. She smiled shyly. "I'm Amy Anderson.

Nice to meet you, too."

"Serena," Luna whispered into Serena's ear. "Be careful around this girl. I feel a strong aura around her, I think she may be with our Enemies."

"What?" Serena coughed.

Amy looked up from checking her watch. "What did you say?" she asked.

Serena turned bright red and giggled. "Oh, nothing," she said as she covered Luna's face with her hand. "This dumb kitty of mine keeps bugging me to feed her. She's really more like a pig than a cat."

Luna muttered angrily from beneath Serena's palm, but Serena ignored it.

"Anyway, Amy, wanna hang for a bit? I kinda bombed that test today, and I wanna put off facing my mom."

Amy brushed a strand of hair from her face and smiled. "Alright," she answered. "Where do you like to go after school most days? The library?"

Serena's eyes widened. "Library?" she repeated slowly, cocking an eyebrow. "Um, Amy, are you feeling OK?"

"Fine. Why?"

mercury rising

Serena shook her head and whistled. "I only know of dweebs that go to the library for fun. I'm not even sure I know where the place is, and I've lived here my whole life."

Amy turned pink and covered her mouth. "Oh," she mumbled. "I'm sorry, I just like to read in my spare time."

Serena was immediately overwhelmed with pity for the slim brainiac. *Read books? For fun?* If it wasn't a comic book, Serena didn't consider it worth reading.

Well, she thought, this book she was in was an exception.

"C'mon, Amy," Serena said, linking arms with her. "You definitely need to get out. I'll take you to the arcade for a few games to relax that huge brain of yours."

"Arcade?" Amy asked. "I'm afraid I've never played video games before."

Serena winced. "Oh, Amy. You seriously need to get out more. C'mon."

Serena took Amy's hand, and the two girls made their way down the sidewalk toward the Crown Arcade.

"No! You stupid...no! Hey, stop shooting. Stop. Stop! What?! NO!"

Serena slammed her fists into the *Sailor V* game in disgust. "This thing is rigged!" she shouted. "I lost again."

Geez, Serena thought angrily. She spent all her allowance on this stupid game every week and she never got any better. The game could at least show a little sympathy and let her get past level 2.

"OK, Amy," Serena sighed as got off the stool. "Your turn."

Amy froze. "Me?" she whispered. "Oh, Serena, I couldn't."

"Why not?" Serena replied as she settled Amy on the stool. "You've been watching me play for the past ten minutes, so you should get the controls." She grinned. "Besides, a little exposure to healthy activities should be good for you."

Amy's eyes focused on the blinking screen, and she took a breath. She pulled a quarter from her skirt pocket and slipped it into the coin slot.

"Thank you for helping Sailor V continue her plight against the scum of the world," the game unit said. Sailor V popped up on the screen, and Amy gripped the joystick. She pushed the FIRE button, and Sailor V blasted away an ogre.

"Good!" Serena commended. "Good, Amy. Keep that up, you may one day even get as good as I am."

"Not much of a challenge," Luna murmured from Serena's feet. Serena responded by bouncing a quarter off Luna's head.

Soon enough, Amy passed onto the next level. And the next. And the next.

Serena's eyes widened. Level 13? "Gee, Amy," Serena said. "You're really doing good."

Amy passed level 13, then 14, then 15. Serena started to sweat. Amy's score was reaching 10,000 points, and she'd never seen anyone break 15,000.

Serena heard mumbling around her. She turned to see a crowd had formed around them.

"Wow," a voice exclaimed from the back of the mob. "Did that new girl just get 12,000 points?"

Serena recognized the voice.

"Andrew!" Serena called, smiling brightly and waving. "Hi!"

Andrew Foreman worked at the arcade—Serena had a MAJOR crush on him.

"Hey, Serena. Man, that girl just got 15,000!"

Serena wilted. She hardly ever got to come to the arcade and see Andrew, and now her chance was going to be ruined because of Amy's point-racking fest.

No fair, she whined to herself. She'd spent five bucks in quarters and didn't even get 1,000 points. Brainy people have all the luck.

Amy was just blasting away a huge dragon when she suddenly gasped and checked her watch. "Oh my God!" she exclaimed as she jumped up. "I'm gonna be late for cram school!"

Amy forgot about the game, and Sailor V was crushed under the dragon's foot.

Amy pushed her way through the crowd to get to the arcade door, but the mob was too busy marveling at her first place score to move. Amy tripped and fell. Serena ran to Amy to help collect her things.

"Oh, Serena." Amy gasped. "I'm so late for cram school! What am I going to do?"

"Oh, being late's not so bad," Serena said as

she collected Amy's pencils and put them in their case. "You get used to it."

"But this Crystal Seminar Cram School is special," Amy explained as she threw her books in her bag. "We study after school every day in order to prepare for our SAT's, and the teacher's really strict."

Serena shook her head. A different school, after normal school was out? What kind of a girl would put herself through that torture? Maybe Amy needed something besides video games prescribed for her.

Amy grabbed her book bag and jumped up. "Thanks for bringing me here, Serena, it was fun!" she called as she ran out the door and down the sidewalk.

Serena walked out the door to wave good-bye, but Amy had already disappeared.

"Hmm." Serena frowned. "Running to go to extra schooling. That poor girl."

"Maybe you could learn or thing or two about responsibility from her," Luna murmured as she walked outside to join the blond.

"That's a good one, Luna," Serena answered

sarcastically. "I don't wanna go to any more school than I absolutely have to."

The doors of the Crown Arcade slid open, and Andrew ran out. "Serena!" he cried. "Oh, I'm so glad I found you!"

Serena's eyes widened. "Really?" she exclaimed, cartoon hearts practically popping out of her head. "Oh, Andrew, I'm so glad you're here!"

Andrew smiled and held out a disk. "Your friend dropped this. Can you can give it to her?"

A train smashed full force into Serena--at least, that was what it felt like.

"Sure." Serena gritted her teeth. "It'd be a pleasure."

Andrew patted her on the head. "Thanks a ton, Serena," he called as he walked back inside.

Serena sighed and looked at the disk. Why was it Amy was diverting hottie Andrew's attention without even trying?

"Brainy people," she mumbled again. "They have all the luck."

Chapter 7
Crystal
Clear Plot

At Crystal Seminar Cram School, Amy rummaged through her bag desperately.

"Oh, no," she exclaimed. "My disk's not here! Did I drop it at the arcade?" She sighed nervously. "First I'm late, and now this."

"Amy?" The professor was a tall woman, with wavy brown hair and glasses over brown eyes. She smiled. "How's my star student?"

"Oh--Professor!" Amy blurted, turning red. "I'm fine, ma'am."

The professor patted Amy's shoulder. "Good to hear." She purred. "As our model student, I'm pleased to see you take your studies seriously."

"Yes," Amy mumbled.

"Now, please use your special Crystal Disk to do all your work on." The woman's eyes flickered. "I want to see you use that disk as much as you can."

"Of course, Professor."

The tall woman nodded, then moved away to check on the other students. Amy breathed a sigh of relief and turned back to the G3 PowerBook she had set up at her desk.

"When I find my disk, I suppose I'll use it," Amy said quietly as she booted up the laptop. She frowned. "Though I'm not sure I want to. It always gives me a headache, for some reason."

Amy sighed and pulled out a notebook from her book bag. "Well, without it I might as well start my homework the old-fashioned way," she said as she took one of her pens and began to write down advanced chemistry equations.

Amy didn't see the Professor's eyes light up as she watched all the students working diligently. The woman smirked.

"Yes," the Professor whispered wickedly.

"Yes, little students, use those disks until they drain all your energy. The Negaverse will thrive with your power!"

She laughed. "Master Jedite, your flawless plan will lead the Negaverse to rule the world!"

Serena yawned as she walked down the street with Luna. The sun was hot, and Serena had just dealt with a full day of school and a rigorous video gaming session. She was definitely ready for a nap.

"Luna," she said. "Could you just go to this cram school place and bring Amy her disk without me? I need my beauty sleep."

Luna shook her head. "We need to check this place out, Serena. I've read advertisements about the school, and they insist their special Crystal Disks will turn anyone into a genius."

"Really?" Serena's eyes widened as she examined the disk in her hand. It looked normal enough. But could it turn her into a genius?

"Hey," she laughed happily. "Maybe I don't need to bum test answers from Amy after all. If I use this disk, I'll get as smart as she is in no time, and I can ace my tests and bust the Sailor V game!"

Luna growled. "I mean it sounds suspicious, Serena! And remember, Amy is very likely working with our Enemy."

Serena snorted. "That's ridiculous, Luna. Amy's probably the gentlest person I ever met. She may be a little anti-social, but she's definitely not evil."

"I find it amazing you call anyone who doesn't play Sailor V 24-7 anti-social," Luna muttered. "But I definitely feel a strong aura around Amy, and that's usually a tell-tale sign someone is working with the Enemy."

"That aura's probably just her massive brain waves," Serena answered as she entertained herself by tossing the disk into the air. "And I'm checking out this disk. I'm willing to try any short-cut to become a genius."

Luna scowled. "A miracle couldn't make you a genius, Serena."

Serena whipped her head at her cat. "That's not funny!" she snapped back. "You think that just because I don't study or pay attention in class or do any homework there's no way that I could become--"

"That's a really productive schedule, blondie."

Serena swung around. "Oh, great." She snarled. "It's you."

Sure enough, it was her dark-haired, fashion-conscious nemesis. Today he was decked out in Abercrombie's finest, with his traditional Oakleys.

"It's no wonder you get such terrible grades," he said mockingly. "Not only do you pig-out constantly and rot your brain with comic books, you talk to your cat."

Serena clenched her fists. "At least my cat can hold a better conversation than you can!"

How *dare* he just walk out of nowhere and insult her! This jerk needed to get a life.

Pretty-boy lowered his shades and focused ocean blue eyes on her. "I'd normally make fun of you for that comment," he said quietly, "but I'm pretty sure a moment ago I heard that cat talk."

Serena froze, and Luna tensed by her side. had he heard Luna talking?

Serena began to laugh loudly, though her

cheeks turned red. "That's ridiculous!" she shouted through her laughter. "Cats can't talk! You're so stupid! HAHAHA!"

Serena grabbed Luna, turned around, and ran away like lightning. She felt the guy's eyes on her as she dashed away, so she just ran faster. Two blocks later she finally stopped and fell to the ground.

"Oh my God, that was close," Serena panted. "Geez, Luna--you gotta stop that mouth of yours. If a dork like that guy heard you talk, you must be blabbing in public too often."

Luna let out a breath and shook her head. "That was close. Well, at least he's gone." The cat looked up and saw a computer store.

"Hey, Serena," Luna said. "Let's go in there and check out that disk. There may be something on it that can tell us who Amy really is."

"Aw," Serena complained, examining the disk. "I don't know how to use this thing! Floppy disks are so ancient. It's all CD's and the Internet now."

"Kids who do their homework know how to use disks," Luna answered shortly.

mercury rising

Serena shook her head as the two of them walked through the store's sliding glass doors. Luna was getting as bad as her mother, Serena thought. Maybe even worse, and that was saying a lot.

Luna hopped onto a display table where a new desktop Mac was hooked up. "Stick the disk in the slot, Serena."

Serena obeyed, and Luna immediately began typing on the keyboard.

"Wow," Serena commented. "I didn't know you could use a computer, Luna." She also thought Luna looked kind of funny typing away like a human, but decided not to say that.

"They're real user-friendly nowadays," Luna answered as she clicked the mouse. Something popped up on the screen, and the computer emitted a screeching noise.

"Hey!" Serena shouted, covering her ears. "Luna, what'd you do?"

Luna's eyes widened. "I knew it!" she exclaimed. "This is a brainwashing program!" She clicked the mouse vigorously and the disk slid out. The noise abruptly stopped.

"A what?" Serena let go of her ears and frowned. "What would Amy be doing with a brainwashing program?"

"Put two and two together, Serena," Luna snapped as she flicked red-orange eyes at the girl. "Don't you get it? Amy's working with the Enemy!"

Serena stood outside of Crystal Seminar Cram school, shaking her head. "I still don't believe it," she muttered as she looked up the tall building. "Amy couldn't be working for the Enemy." Serena couldn't forget how sad Amy had looked by herself on the windowsill, and how gently she had pet Luna.

"The disk proves it," Luna replied. "Now use your Luna Pen to get in there so we can stop her from brainwashing all the students."

Serena sighed and pulled out her Luna Pen. She thrust it into the air.

"MOON POWER...TRANSFORM INTO A FASHIONABLE NURSE!"

The traditional pink and orange smoke encircled her body, and when it faded she beamed.

"Wow," Serena exclaimed. "I look great!"

Serena's new outfit consisted of a long lab coat, with a Laura Ashley yellow blouse and knee-length skirt underneath. Her hair was cropped to her shoulders and revealed pearl earrings, and her high heels clicked on the concrete. Very chic, if she did say so herself.

"Follow me, Serena!" Luna cried as she ran into the building. Serena flew after her, and the two dashed up a flight of stairs. When they reached the room with all the students, Serena kicked open the door, Sailor V style.

"There's a medical emergency!" she declared as she ran into the room. "Your disks are hazardous to your health. Stop using them immediately and step away from your computers!"

Amy, at her desk, looked up. "I'm sorry," she said, "but I don't think there's any emergency. Please don't disrupt the students--we're trying to study."

Serena's jaw dropped. All the other students in the room looked half-zombified already, bleary-eyed and weak. Amy was the only one that seemed all right.

It's true! Serena thought. *Amy is working for the Enemy!* And to think, she'd actually felt sorry for her and wanted to be her friend.

"You're lower than I thought, Amy," Nurse Serena spat. "You've been draining all of these kids' energy. How pathetic of you to work for evil scum like Jedite!"

Amy's eyes widened. "What?"

"Don't play innocent. You have to be punished!" Serena raised her hand in the air.

"MOON PRISM POWER MAKE-UP!"

In a display much like those *Disco Fever* reruns on VH-1, swirling colored lights engulfed Nurse Serena. Amy gasped.

"Sailor Moon?"

Sailor Moon put one hand on her hip. "Amy," she shouted. "Your energy-sucking days are over!"

Amy was about to protest when the professor of the class abruptly slapped a hand over her mouth. The tall woman grinned as she gripped Amy's shoulder with long-nailed fingers.

"Well, well, looks like you have the wrong girl." The professor hissed. Her body began to grow taller, and her skin faded from peach to red. In a moment she was no longer a human--she was a demon with piercing black eyes and scraggly black hair.

Serena's eyes widened. "You mean, Amy wasn't the one behind all this?" she asked, though she was pretty sure she knew the answer.

"No." The demon grinned. "She's my hostage now. Prepare to meet your doom, Sailor brat."

Chapter 8
Mercury
Blasts Off

The demon lady gripped Amy tighter and smiled coldly at Serena.

"You're not strong enough to take me on, Sailor girl." She hissed. "I will drain your energy and take over this city in the name of evil!"

But Serena wasn't listening. All she could think was Luna had gotten her upset at Amy for nothing! She felt bad--after all, she had said some pretty mean things to the brainiac who she wanted to be friends with.

"Luna!" the Sailor-suited warrior shouted, stamping her booted foot on the floor. "I told you Amy wasn't evil! Geez, why don't you ever listen to me?"

Luna's eyes were wide. "But I'm sure there's a strong aura about her," the cat murmured.

"Yeah, well, you missed the train on this one!" Serena snarled. "I mean, even if you just went by hair you would've been able to tell."

Luna shook her head. "Serena, what are you talking about?"

"All the villains we've gone against have had awful hair," Serena explained, counting on her fingers. "Like that witch who pretended to be Molly's mom from the first book, and the Godzilla wannabe from *Sailor Moon Novel #2*. Even this fashion-deprived demon-type lady's got hair like a mop." She pointed to the demon's crusty, scraggly black mess of hair.

"But Amy's got great hair. Almost as good as mine." Serena snorted. "No one with such fine taste in hair stylists could be bad, Luna." God, how could Luna have overlooked that?

The demon's red-skinned face turned even redder. "You brat!" she screamed. "How dare you compare my hair to a mop! I'll have you know that in the demon world, my hairdo is considered very in-style!"

"Then remind me to never have my hair done in the demon world!" Serena shot back.

The bad-hair-day demon roared with anger. Amy struggled in her grip, but the demon only held her tighter.

"Time for a pop quiz, Sailor Loser," the demon barked. "Why did the apple fall on Newton's head?"

Serena scowled. "Don't ask me, ask the apple," she spat as she reached for her tiara.

"Wrong! You fail!" The demon shot out a hand, and razor sharp test papers zoomed at Serena full speed. Serena barely dove out of the way in time.

"Woah, those things are sharp," she exclaimed. This is even worse than school, she thought nervously. At least at school no one threw things at her. Well, sometimes Miss Haruna wanted to throw things, but she never actually did. Certainly not razor sharp test papers--probably one of those exclusive-to-the-demon-world things, Serena thought.

"Question number two." The demon kept

up the pace. "Describe gravity in under fifty words."

"Not doing it," Serena yelled as she stood up. "No way I'm playing your stupid game. I don't mind being attacked with daggers and laser beams, but fight me with homework and you make me really mad!"

"Wrong!" The demon sneered. "Slaves, attack this stupid girl. She's giving a bad name to students everywhere!"

All the brainwashed students at their desks began to rise. Serena's eyes widened as she saw them lurch towards her, their arms outstretched, their eyes black.

"Kill...kill..." they chanted.

Serena backed up against the wall, but the students only pressed closer. She screamed as they started to pull at her. "Ew, Luna, help!" she cried. "I can't get my tiara off to de-brainwash them!"

Luna was about to run to Serena, but just then the demon lady grabbed Amy by the hair and shoved her face against a computer screen.

"Didn't use the computer disk like I told you?" The demon growled. "You little upstart!

Now I'll suck all your brain energy dry!"

Amy cried out as her face was squashed against the computer monitor. "I don't need any disk to make me smart." Amy gasped as she tried to break free. "Success at schoolwork comes from the mind, not any new piece of technology!"

Just then, something began to glow on Amy's forehead. The demon narrowed her eyes as a small blue symbol, a heart with antennas perched on a small cross, glowed on Amy's forehead.

Luna's eyes shot open. "That's the symbol of Mercury!" she cried.

The demon threw Amy to the floor. "My brainwashing computer program isn't working on you because you didn't use the disk!" The demon snarled. "So I'll just kill you instead."

Amy gasped.

Luna immediately jumped into the air and spun. Blue lights flashed around her, and when she finally landed, a blue pen with the symbol of Mercury on the top landed with her.

"Amy!" Luna shouted, sliding the pen with all her might. "Take the pen and yell MERCURY POWER MAKE-UP!"

Amy grabbed the pen and turned to Luna with wide eyes. "You can talk, kitty?"

"Just do it!" Luna cried. The demon had changed her arm into a large ax, and was raising it to chop at Amy.

Amy saw the ax and screamed. She thrust the pen into the air and closed her eyes.

"MERCURY POWER MAKE-UP!"

Serena fought out of a brainwashed student's grip, then looked up in disbelief. Blue light flashed through the room, and sparkling ribbons of blue enveloped Amy and melted her clothes into a Sailor Scout uniform.

Serena's jaw dropped. "Amy's a super-hero?!"

Amy looked down at her outfit in shock. It was almost identical to Serena's, only her colors were blue and indigo, and her brooch, earrings, and choker were solid blue.

"She's Sailor Mercury," Luna declared happily. "I knew I felt something about her."

All the brainwashed students turned to the new Scout, and Serena pouted.

"No fair!" Serena complained. "Her transformation sequence is prettier than mine."

It seemed that Amy, even as a Sailor Scout, was going to get all the breaks again.

The demon growled. "Two Sailor brats?" she grumbled. "Now I have to take care of both of you." She raised her ax.

"Mercury!" Luna shouted. "Use your power! MERCURY BUBBLES BLAST!"

Amy took a breath, then cupped her hands together. "MERCURY BUBBLES..." A ball of blue light formed in her palms, and she released it full force. "...BLAST!"

The room was immediately filled with thick bubbles that formed into a fog. The brainwashed students were confused by it, and Serena used the chance to get away from them.

My turn, Serena thought. She couldn't let Amy steal the show like in the arcade, now could she?

"What's going on?" the demon cried. "I can't see anything!"

"Bye-bye, you bad-haired excuse for a demon!" Serena yelled as she pulled off her tiara and flung it through the air.

mercury rising

"MOON TIARA ACTION!"

The demon screamed as the tiara hit her in the stomach. "No!" she cried as she was enveloped by golden light. "A middle school flunky can't do this to me!" In a second the light zapped her body into nothingness, and only a pile of dust remained.

"Hmph." Serena crossed her arms. "I may be a flunky, but at least I'm not a pile of dust on the floor."

The brainwashed students snapped out of their spell, and together they fell to the floor in a heap. Sailor Mercury walked up, eyes wide. "Serena?" she asked, her voice shaky. "Is that you?"

Serena smiled and took Amy's hands. "Sure is. Pretty cool, Amy. I didn't know you could blast villains so well."

"Neither did I," Amy answered, shaking her head in disbelief. "This is odd, I mean, when Luna told me to use my power, for some reason I just knew how."

Serena laughed. "I know. It was the same with me. Don't worry, you get used to all this Champion of Justice stuff soon enough."

Luna walked up, a big smile on her face.

"Excellent work, Amy. You did a great job. Welcome to the team."

Serena giggled. *All right!* she thought. Now that Amy was here, she wouldn't have to work so hard. And Amy was so smart, she'd probably do most of the work anyway.

"But Serena," said Luna, cocking an eyebrow, "I want you to know that just because another Scout is here doesn't mean you can slack off. If anything, you two will need to work harder now to face our enemies."

Serena scowled. She swore that cat could read minds.

"Thanks for making my day, Luna," Serena grumbled.

Amy laughed.

"You know," Serena said the next day, as she and Amy walked home from school. "I really do think you're the smartest girl to ever come to our school, Amy."

Amy blushed. "Thank you, Serena," she replied with a smile.

Luna, on Serena's shoulder, nodded. "Your

intelligence is going to be a valuable asset to the Sailor Scout Team. It should help us become an even stronger force."

Yeah, Serena thought quickly, asset to the team.

"Amy," Serena drawled, taking the thin girl's arm and smiling sweetly. "Now that we're gonna be friends and teammates and all, do you think you could make me a genius?"

Amy smiled. "Why, of course," she answered. "Anyone can become a genius, Serena."

"Woo hoo!" Serena cried, Homer Simpson-style. "I told you, Luna! And you said I'd never be--."

"We'll study every day after school for three hours. Would you like to start tomorrow?"

Serena froze. Luna laughed as the blond turned slowly to the blue-haired girl. "You mean, to be smart I have to study?" Serena croaked.

Amy nodded. "Of course, it's the only way. There's no short cut to becoming good at school, Serena."

Serena moaned and grabbed her head. "No way!" she cried. "You can't just tell me the answers to the tests?"

Amy frowned. "That would be cheating, Serena."

Serena fell to her knees. All that kissing up to Amy, and now she couldn't become a genius without studying?

Oh, well, Serena thought with a sigh. She was glad they were friends anyway. Amy was cool. And here Serena thought all brainiacs were dorks.

"So," Amy asked. "Do you want me to help you study, Serena?"

"Nah," Serena answered. "That much studying could make me sick. I have a weak brain."

Luna rolled her eyes.

"But there is one thing," Serena remarked. "Do you think you could help me with something else?"

"What?" Amy asked.

Serena grinned. "Teach me how to beat the *Sailor V* game!"

Chapter 9
Tick Tock,
I Wanna
Buy the Clock!

"Jedite!"

Jedite flicked golden-blond hair from his eyes nervously. Stepping out from the shadows, he bowed on one knee.

"You called, my queen?" he asked as he kept his gaze to the stone floor.

Queen Beryl's eyes glinted dangerously. Her long nails flashed as she clenched her fist.

"Your failures are starting to annoy me, Jedite." She hissed. The darkness of the Negaverse thumped around her, as if the hot air itself joined in her anger. Shadows swirled around her fiery red hair.

"Forgive me, my queen." Jedite hesitantly looked up. "That brat Sailor Moon--"

"Just got a little friend!" Queen Beryl cut him off with a wave of her hand. "She should not have posed a problem for you, general, yet you failed to destroy her. Now there is another Sailor Scout. What do you intend to do about it?"

"My main priority is to gather the energy you request, my queen," Jedite answered softly. "Neither Sailor Moon nor her new partner will stop me in my newest plan."

Queen Beryl's eyes narrowed. "For your sake, I hope you are right. I need that energy, general, and I need it now."

"Of course." Jedite lowered his head. "My life is for you only, my queen. I will get started at once."

"Mall day, mall day, la, la, la!"

Serena hopped through the mall like a pleased rabbit, her ponytails bouncing behind her. A very hesitant Amy followed.

"Uh, Serena? People are staring. Your

singing's a little loud."

"What's the fun in shopping if you can't enjoy yourself, Ams!" Serena declared as she took another lick of her Baskin Robbins cheesecake ice cream. She was wearing her favorite outfit--Gap overalls and a Boy Joy floppy hat fitted snugly over her hair buns. An Illusion necklace hung around her neck, and body glitter sparkled on her face. Serena was chic and ready for a fabulous shopping spree!

"You seem in a good mood, Serena," Amy muttered as she avoided passing people's stares.

Serena laughed. "It's gonna be a great day, Amy, I can feel it. My horoscope said I'd find something earth-shattering in my shopping today."

Amy frowned. "Horoscopes aren't really something to go by, Serena." She waved her finger at Serena. "They have no scientific backing to them. The stars' movements have no bearing on the way we act or the way the world affects us."

Serena turned to Amy with narrowed eyes. "You sound like my science teacher, Amy," she said lowly. "The whole reason I come to the mall is to forget about school."

"Oh." Amy blushed. "I'm sorry, it's just...I've never been to the mall before."

"Geez," Serena mumbled as she bit into her ice cream cone. "I still don't understand how you've stayed alive fourteen years without playing video games or mall trotting. It's like you grew up in a bubble or something!"

Serena really enjoyed Amy's company, but she was often a little frustrated by the blue-haired girl's lack of funness. Amy was smart and nice, but no fun at a party.

As if anyone could have a fulfilling life without fudge sundaes or video games, Serena thought as her eyes searched the surrounding stores. She wanted to find a place that'd show Amy there was more to life than homework.

"Oh!" Amy suddenly cried out and pointed. "Look, Serena, a book store. Can we go in there?"

Serena gagged. Books? Ew, education!

But then Serena saw the huge *Sailor V* comic book poster in the window.

"Great idea," she declared as she grabbed Amy's wrist and dragged the girl inside. "Borders Books and Music it is. But let me show you around, OK?"

Borders had several display stands set up near the door for New York Times Bestsellers, Sale Books, and New Titles. Serena walked past them without even a glance.

"Here," the blond declared as she stopped in front of a large shelf marked COMICS. "Your one-stop shopping spot. Need some help choosing titles, Amy?"

Amy stared at the shelf with wide eyes. "Comic books?" She pulled one off the shelf and flipped through it. She covered her mouth with a hand.

"But Serena, it's all pictures," she remarked breathlessly. "Aren't you a little old for pictures?"

"It's not *pictures*, it's artful story-telling!" Serena shot back. "Motionless Picture Entertainment. And comic books are better than books with just plain old words in them."

Geez, it was like Amy didn't know any-thing. Comic books weren't kids stuff--they were for sophisticated, creative minds! That was what Serena believed, anyway.

"Besides," Serena added as she pulled the

comic from Amy's hands, "this one isn't any good. A lot of this stuff's not your style, you need a master to show you the gems."

Serena held her chin and let her eyes trail over the bindings. Let's see, she thought. Was Amy a chicks-with-big-swords girl, or a chicks-with-cool-magic girl?

"*Sailor V* is a perfect start," Serena announced as she pulled down a few books and tossed them at Amy. "I think also *Magic Knight Rayearth 1-3* and the first *Sushi Girl* should do it. I'd get you *Gundam*, but I don't think you're a giant robot fan."

Amy stared at the graphic novels Serena had picked, then smiled hesitantly. "All right, I'll try them," she said at last. "Thank you. You've recommended some of your favorites to me, may I do the same for you?"

"Huh?"

Amy smiled and took Serena's hand. After zigzagging through a few sections, Amy at last stood in front of a large shelf. The sign read MATH AND SCIENCE, and Serena choked.

"Advanced Algebra is my favorite." Amy

giggled as she pulled a thick book down and held it up. "It's so fascinating! All the numbers fit together like a puzzle, and you can figure out almost anything."

Good God, Serena thought. She enjoys math.

"That's it." Serena yanked the book out of Amy's hands and shoved it back on the shelf. She took the girl firmly by the shoulders.

"Listen to me," Serena said lowly. "We are not in school. It's Saturday. School isn't going to be here for another day. We shouldn't be thinking about school or doing anything related to school until we are in school."

"But--"

"No 'buts!'" Serena dragged Amy out of the store. "We need to get out of this place, it holds potential educational dangers."

Amy sighed.

Serena led Amy on a long trek through the mall, stopping in clothing shops and jewelry boutiques. Serena bought a new shirt at Abercrombie and a new ring at Claire's, though Amy only purchased a soft pretzel at Pretzel Time. She tried to get Serena to stop in another bookstore, but Serena refused.

"I'm doing this for your own good, Ams," Serena explained as she half-dragged the thin girl from Waldenbooks. "I want you to relax." I also have a major itch to find that cool thing my horoscope said I'd come across, she added to herself. Maybe it's a fab new sweater, or a rockin' video game, or a donut the size of a mini-van!

Serena hoped it was the donut.

A store with huge banners and balloons suddenly caught her eye. The words GRAND OPENING SUPER SALE danced across the top of the doorway in fancy letters.

"Mall lesson number one," Serena instructed as she pointed to the shop. "SALE is the magic word. We're going in."

It was a clock store called TICKING TREA-SURES. It was very new, Serena had been to the mall the week before, and it hadn't been there. She gaped as she walked in the doorway.

Clocks of every shape, size, and color were lined up on the walls and counters. They all ticked together, making Serena feel oddly dizzy as she stepped through and looked around. Cuckoos popped out of a few of them and chirped loudly.

"These are gorgeous!" Serena exclaimed happily. "I've never seen such wicked clocks!" She picked up one in the shape of a sad mushroom man and laughed. "Amy, check this out."

Amy giggled. "My, he looks tired." The mushroom man's eyes were drooping and red. She patted him on the head. "I'd say you needed another five minutes before getting up this morning," she murmured with a smile.

"Look, Amy." Serena pointed to a clock shaped like a slice of pizza. "That's something I'd love to have on my wall."

"It's you, Serena." Amy laughed as she picked up another clock. "And look at this one."

Amy's clock was in the shape of a black cat. Serena's eyes widened.

"It looks just like Luna," she remarked as she looked at its back. "And it's pretty cheap. Maybe I should get it so Luna'll have some company."

"Luna would probably just get jealous," Amy said, and they both laughed.

"Can I help you girls?" The clerk, an older

woman with stylish curly hair and a velvet choker walked up to Serena and Amy. "All clocks are 50% off the ticket price."

"That's so cheap," Serena cried as she took the cat clock from Amy and looked it over. Maybe this clock was what her horoscope was talking about, Serena thought. If that was the case, she couldn't ignore the command of the stars--Serena was great at finding excuses to buy stuff.

"I'll take this one," Serena announced as she handed the clock to the clerk. "I'm late for school every day--maybe this'll help me quit getting detentions." Plus, the Dumbo clock her mom had bought her when she was four was getting really embarrassing.

"Serena, I'm afraid you don't have enough," Amy noted. "You have very little money left after buying that shirt."

Serena gasped and checked her purse. She pulled out the money she had left and groaned.

"You're right," she mumbled sadly. "Oh, man, now I'll never get to school on time. I practically hold the record for most tardies in our school's history as it is."

"If you have trouble waking up in the morning," Amy said, "I could help out. If I pick you up at 7:30 we should get there no problem."

"You'd really pick me up in the morning?" Serena asked. "You'd do that for me?"

Amy giggled and cocked her head to one side. "Of course I would. You're my friend, Serena, it'd be my pleasure."

Serena brightened. Amy's so nice! she thought. We've only known each other for a week and she's already treating me like a life-long friend.

"Sounds like a plan," Serena replied with a grin. "I can't say I really wanna get to school earlier than I have to, but being on time sure beats staying after and wiping the boards."

Amy scratched her cheek. "Miss Haruna really makes you wipe the boards?"

Serena giggled wickedly. "Yeah, though while I do it she always moans about how terrible her love life is. I swear, I know the names of all the guys she ever went out with, and all the ways they dumped her!"

The two girls laughed as they chatted on about their pathetically single teacher and walked out the door. Once they'd gone, the clerk snarled.

"Leave without a clock, will you?" She growled under her breath. "No matter. I'll get your energy soon enough."

The woman's green eyes flickered a bottom-less, glittering black.

Chapter 10
Cupcake Break

"I'm home, Mom!" Serena called as she stepped into her doorway and slipped off her shoes. "Is dinner ready? I'm starving."

"You're always starving," Sammy muttered as he walked by with a comic book. Serena scowled as he made himself comfortable on the couch.

"And you're always a brat," she snapped. "That'd better not be one of mine."

"Like I'd wanna read any of your comics," Sammy shot back as he looked at her through narrowed eyes. "This is quality giant-robot material, not your silly girls-with-big-swords stuff."

Serena's eyes blazed. "Don't you dare dis my Rayearth!"

"Please, please," Mrs. Tsukino pleaded as she walked in the room. "No bickering, kids. Your father's had a long day."

Serena crossed her arms angrily. "But Mom, he was insulting my taste!"

She wished she could morph into Sailor Moon and teach him a lesson. Then she'd show him. *I am Sailor Moon, Champion of Justice and defender of girls' comics everywhere, and in the name of the moon, you're punished!*

"Relax, dear." Serena's mother comforted her as she steered the girl into the kitchen. "I made some cupcakes for you."

Serena immediately forgot about punishing her brother as soon as she saw the double-frosted chocolate cupcakes. The little rainbow sprinkles on top caught the light and glittered like gems.

Serena shoved an entire one in her mouth before her mother could blink. She grinned as she attempted chewing. "Fanks, mom!"

Mrs. Tsukino's eyes widened. "Goodness,

dear, slow down! You'll choke if you eat it all at once."

Her mom didn't have to worry, Serena thought proudly as she swallowed. Serena was a pro at scarfing. She picked up another cupcake and smiled. "OK, Mom."

Mrs. Tsukino grinned and pulled a box from behind her back. "I was just at the mall a few minutes ago, and I found this wonderful store," she explained. "They were selling clocks at high discount, so I picked up a few. Here's yours."

Serena's eyes widened. She accepted the red-wrapped box and ripped off the paper. When she opened it, she cried out and sprayed the air with cupcake crumbs.

It was the cat clock.

"Oh my God, what a coincidence!" Serena cried as she lifted it up. "I was just at the mall, and I wanted to buy this. I must've just missed you."

Serena was kind of glad she had missed her mother. She loved her and all, but hanging with your mom at the mall was definitely not cool.

As Serena happily hugged the clock, she remembered her horoscope. That must've been the special thing she was supposed to find!

"Thanks so much, Mom," Serena called as she grabbed the plate of cupcakes and ran up the stairs. She burst through her bedroom door and yelled, "Luna, wake up!"

Luna was on Serena's bed, napping as usual. She opened her eyes groggily. "Mmm, what is it?" she mumbled.

"And you say I sleep too much." Serena sat next to Luna and held out the clock. "I got you a buddy. What do you think?"

Luna blinked the sand from her eyes and looked at the clock. She frowned, then lowered her head back down. "I like the Dumbo one better."

"Ah, you're no fun," Serena spat as she set the clock up on her bedside table. "I thought this clock looked like you, so you might--"

"It does not look like me!" Luna exclaimed indignantly. "That ugly thing has beady little eyes and an evil smile. I can't believe you want to fall asleep with it next to your bed."

Serena sighed and shook her head. "Amy was right," she said. "You are jealous."

"I am not!"

mercury rising

"Anyway," Serena continued, "with any luck this thing'll wake me up in time to meet Amy tomorrow morning and I'll finally start getting to school on time." She cocked an eyebrow. "That should make you happy."

Luna yawned. "If that thing can get you to school on time," she remarked, "then I'll eat my food dish."

Serena laughed. Wow, wouldn't that be great to see!

"Don't forget you said that, Luna," Serena said with a wicked grin. She picked up a video game cartridge from her desk and got up.

"What are you doing?"

"Gonna go play video games at Molly's," Serena explained as she grabbed another cupcake and shoved it in her mouth. Mall trotting, a new clock, double-chocolate cupcakes, video games-- this was turning out to be an excellent day. And if Luna ended up eating her food dish tomorrow, Serena would declare this the best week ever.

Luna sat up. "Wait," she called as Serena began to leave. "Serena, didn't you have home-work that you had to do--"

But Serena was already long gone, leaving only a few cupcake crumbs on the floor behind her.

Luna crinkled up her nose angrily. "Geez. Why do I even try with that girl?" Her eyes flicked to the empty plate, and she frowned.

"She could've at least left me a cupcake," the cat muttered as she lowered her head on her paws.

That night, Luna was awakened by Serena's snoring, as usual.

"Serena." The cat growled as she covered her ears with her paws. Her red-orange eyes lifted angrily to see Serena sprawled on her bed. The girl slept with one leg hanging off the side, her arms spread, and her tongue hanging out of her grinning mouth. She snored again, making Luna wince.

"That girl's louder than a vacuum cleaner," the cat murmured as she rubbed the sleep from her eyes. She stood up. "The only way I'm going to sleep tonight is by going to Sammy's room."

Suddenly, Serena's new cat clock began to glow. Luna watched as the cat's beady eyes lit up with yellow light. The light throbbed, then shot out to wash over the sleeping Serena.

"What?" Luna jumped onto the bedside table and examined the clock. The light didn't appear to be hurting Serena, she was snoring just as loudly as before. Still, Luna didn't like the look of it.

"That doesn't seem like any kind of alarm," the cat remarked. She narrowed her eyes. "There's something very strange about this clock."

"Yummy!" Serena cried out in her sleep happily. "Oh, Andrew, this huge sundae just for me? You're such a darling!"

Luna rolled her eyes. "I'll deal with it in the morning," she muttered as she walked out the door. "I have to get some sleep in order to think straight, and I sure won't get any sleep in here."

Luna left the room, and Serena was left to drooling, giggling, and snoring in dreamland. The yellow light washed over her again, but she didn't feel a thing.

The cat clock's eyes flickered red.

Amy rapped politely on Serena's door and checked her watch. 7:30 on the dot.

"With any luck, Luna won't have to drag her

out of bed," she said as she swung her book bag. "I wonder what Miss Haruna will think when Serena's actually on time today."

There was a rattling and the door opened. A very cheerful Mrs. Tsukino beamed.

"Amy!" she cried. "Well, what a pleasant surprise. So nice to see you."

Amy nodded her head and smiled. "Hello," she answered. "I'm here for Serena. Is she up yet?"

"Oh, I'm afraid Serena left a long time ago," Mrs. Tsukino said quickly. "Yes, out the door by 7 a.m. That girl's such a trooper. Off to school, running, a half-hour ago. Off to school. Shouldn't you be going, Amy? You'll be late, you know." Mrs. Tsukino looked at Amy expectantly. She'd said everything in a few seconds, talking breathlessly and very fast. It was like listening to Serena after she'd drunk too much Surge.

"She's already gone?!" Amy was surprised. "But school doesn't start until 8:30."

"Off, off, you'll be late!" Mrs. Tsukino insisted, turning Amy around and giving her a nudge toward the sidewalk. "Hurry, hurry, don't be late. I have so many things to do, laundry, dishes, dusting, I have to get started. Hurry, hurry!"

Amy tried to turn around, but Mrs. Tsukino was as hyper as a Chihuahua. Before Amy could do anything, she was shoved onto the sidewalk and the door was slammed shut behind her.

Amy gazed at the door with wide eyes. "What was *that* all about?" Amy shook her head. "And Serena, off to school by seven? That's odd. I hope nothing's wrong."

Chapter 11
Rush Hour

By 7:31, half of Serena's homeroom class had shown up. Kids ran in every minute, crying apologies for being late.

"Oh my God!" Molly stood up from her desk and pointed to her watch. "It's 7:32, and we're still missing people!"

"No!" Lisa slammed her fist against her desk. "Where are they? We have to get things started. We have to hurry, hurry, hurry!"

Serena was the worst. She was more impatient than everyone, and more hyper than her mother. It was like she had downed a two-liter bottle of Surge with three pieces of chocolate cake and an entire bowl of sugar.

"I hate waiting!" she cried, grabbing her head. "Where is everyone? And they always yell at me for being late! This is ridiculous, we've been waiting forever!"

"Ahh!" Molly jumped up and down and pointed at her watch. "7:33!"

"That's it." Serena pushed back her chair and grabbed her empty lunch bag. "I already ate my lunch so there's nothing left to do. Molly, Lisa, Melvin, let's go get everyone!"

Her three friends jumped up immediately. "Good idea."

"Every moment we're wasting precious time." Melvin squeaked, wiping sweat from his forehead. "We have to hurry!"

"Hurry, hurry, hurry!" the rest of the students chanted as they jumped up. "We have to hurry, hurry, hurry!"

Miss Haruna was pacing at the front of the room and staring at the clock. At last she threw out her arms.

"Never mind, don't get them," she sputtered. "Just go home and study. It's 7:34, and we're missing 10 students. I'm sick of wasting time! I have a date at 8 tonight, and I can't be late."

"Fine!" Serena shouted. She ran out the door and left the school as fast she could. The rest of the students did the same, and ran off in the direction of their own houses.

Wasting so much time! Serena thought angrily as she flew down the sidewalk. She'd been at that school for more than half an hour, doing nothing. She had to hurry, or nothing would get done!

Serena ran down the sidewalk like lightning, rising a cloud of dust behind her.

Amy stared at all the people running down the street. Kids, teenagers, adults--everyone was dashing about like the world was about to end. It was worse than the last time Pokémon Cards were on sale.

"My goodness," Amy exclaimed as a man in a business suit flew by her. "Everyone's in such a rush for no reason." She frowned and brushed a strand of hair behind her ear. "It feels like something's wrong, it's like the city's in a panic. I hope it's not the Y2K bug again."

"Amy!"

Amy turned around, and her eyes widened. "Luna?"

Luna ran up, panting heavily. The small cat had managed to tie Serena's new clock to her back.

"Serena's house is like a circus." Luna panted. "Her father was out the door by 5 this morning, and Sammy and Serena were out by 7. Serena's mom's been doing chores like a crazed clean-freak all day without resting. She's like the Energizer bunny, only with a mop!"

Amy crouched down and quickly untied the clock from around Luna. "This city's going mad," Amy said. "I've never seen everyone like this."

She picked up the clock to examine it closely. "Hey," she said, "this is that clock Serena wanted from that new store. She got it?"

"Her mother bought it," Luna answered. "And she wasn't the only one, I saw lots of people walking home with boxes from that store yesterday. Last night, that clock emitted a strange light over Serena. I think the clocks are responsible for the city's frenzy."

Amy nodded. "Let's check it out." She and Luna carefully stepped into a park to avoid all the dashing people. They found a bench to sit on. Amy set her book bag on the ground and prepared to open the clock.

"Wait." Luna put her paw on Amy's hand, stopping her. Amy looked up and saw the cat wink. "I have something that'll help," Luna announced as she jumped into the air and flipped.

Indigo lights flashed from the cat. Amy gasped as a small blue compact formed in the air and dropped into her lap. The symbol of Mercury was stamped in gold on the front.

"What's this?" she asked as she flipped it open. There was a tiny keyboard inside, and a screen where the mirror should be.

"It's your Mercury Compact Computer," Luna answered with a grin. "It'll help you scan almost anything."

Amy brightened. "Thank you, Luna! This looks almost as good as my PowerBook."

"It's better. Try it."

Amy nodded and propped the cat clock in

her lap. She typed something into the computer and waited.

Lights flashed on the tiny screen in a rapid display of numbers and symbols. The computer processed its data in a few seconds, then beeped and gave a final reading.

"Oh my God." Amy covered her mouth. "Luna, this is incredible--it just picked up evil energy levels from this clock!"

Luna's eyes narrowed. "I thought so," she said flatly. "Open it up, Amy."

Amy closed the compact and slipped it in her pocket, then gripped the back of the clock. She held her breath and pulled.

A flash of eerie yellow light shot out of the back compartment and zoomed by Amy's cheek. Amy turned around, but the light just flashed into the air and disappeared into the sky.

"What was that?"

Luna peered into the back of the clock, but it was empty. "That light that just shot out was the same light that poured over Serena last night," the cat said lowly. "It's got to be behind this sudden panic in the city."

"Our enemies are doing it." Amy nodded quickly. "That's got to be it!"

In the center of the mall, TICKING TREA-SURES was boarded up. The people rushing through the mall hardly noticed that inside the closed store, someone was laughing evilly.

"Excellent." Jedite rubbed his gloved hands together and walked around the inside of the shop. The store was empty, no clocks, no shelves, no nothing—except for the swirling mass of glowing white light.

"This shop is our base," he told the sorceress who stood off to his left. "All the energy those humans waste by rushing collects here. See it in the very air?" He reached up and let his fingers weave through the thick white light.

He smiled. "Queen Beryl shall take this energy and use it to lead the Negaverse to victory."

The sorceress nodded. She had been the clerk in the TICKING TREASURES, but now her hair had grown dark and fell beyond her shoulders in tangled waves. Her skin was white as milk, her eyes were midnight and glittering.

mercury rising

Jedite turned to her and raised a golden eyebrow. "I must warn you, though. Sailor Moon and her little pal may try to stop you. You've done well so far, but don't botch the job when they show up."

The sorceress smiled thin blue lips. "Worry not, master Jedite," she whispered in a scratchy voice. "I will take care of them."

"Good. Don't fail me." With that, Jedite opened up a portal, stepped inside, and disappeared.

Serena clenched her hands over the bus seat in frustration. All the cars were in a rush, so the bus she was on was stuck in major traffic.

Forever! Serena thought angrily. Everything's taking forever. She had to keep moving! She was wasting time just sitting here. She had to hurry, hurry, hurry!

"Hey!" Serena shouted at the bus driver. "Can't you get moving any faster?"

The other people in the bus were as impatient as Serena, and they all shouted agreement.

"Be quiet!" The bus driver snarled. "I'm in too much of a rush to deal with you. I'm trying to get out of traffic."

Trying wasn't good enough! Serena was a busy girl and she didn't have time to waste. She ignored the DO NOT STAND WHILE BUS IS IN MOTION sign and ran to the front.

"I wanna get off!" she shouted. "I can get home faster if I walk."

The bus turned suddenly, sending Serena crashing to the floor. She bumped her head on a seat.

"Oww!" she cried as she grabbed the forming lump. Serena could practically hear Luna in her ear, yelling, "Serena, the sign tells you not to stand up for a reason. Why don't you ever follow directions?"

She didn't have time to follow directions. She was in a hurry, and everything was wasting her time! She had to get off this bus!

Just then, Serena saw her bus stop zoom by.

"Hey, Mr. Slowpoke!" Serena cried at the driver. "You just missed my stop! What do you think you're doing?"

"Be quiet, little girl!" he shouted back. "I'm in too much of a hurry to stop. I'm going to the last

118

stop without a break!"

Serena's face turned red with anger. "I'm not a little girl!" she yelled. "I'm a stylin' teenage female with important things to do! LET ME OFF THIS BUS!"

The bus driver swerved to avoid hitting another car, and the bus crashed into a telephone poll. Serena was flung down the aisle, where she bumped her head again.

"This isn't funny," she said through gritted teeth. "Any more bumps and I'm gonna look like stylin' teenage cottage cheese."

All the passengers started yelling at the bus driver, and he angrily opened the door.

"Out!" he shouted. "Everybody get out, I'm in a hurry and I can't deal with all of you!"

Serena scrambled up and dashed to the front. "Thanks for wasting so much of my precious time!" she shouted as she jumped out of the bus. She looked around at all the cars and people zooming by.

"This city's a beehive," she muttered angrily. "Everybody's clogging up the streets. I have to get home, but all these people are gonna waste my time. I have to run!" She re-shouldered her back-pack and prepared to dash.

A hand on her shoulder stopped her. "Serena!" a familiar voice cried.

Serena turned around. "Amy," she exclaimed. "Luna! What are you doing here?"

Luna was by Amy's feet. "Serena, the Enemy is making everybody panic," she said quickly. "Amy used her new computer and found that everybody running around is slowly having their energy drained into that clock shop in the mall. Those clocks were what made everybody hurry in the first place."

Serena's eyes widened. "Those creeps!" she cried. "How dare they use adorable products to trick the city. It's like what they did with those Shaneeras in the last novel!" Serena frowned. "Only the Shaneeras weren't really cute at all."

"Let's get to the mall," Amy said. "If we can find the enemies there, we can stop them from making the city panic."

"All right, let's go," Serena declared as she began to run. "Don't be slow, Amy, I'm in a hurry! Let's just beat up these bad guys so I don't have to waste any more time on them."

Amy's eyes widened. "Wow," she said as she ran after the blond. "I guess this panicking spell actually has some side benefits. Serena didn't complain about having to fight like she normally does."

Luna jumped on her shoulder and smirked. "Maybe we shouldn't break the spell," she said. "Then Serena'd actually start being on time."

Amy smiled. She shook her head and ran faster after Serena, in the direction of the towering Crossroads Mall.

Chapter 12
Running Out
of Time

The mall was closed by the time they got there. A big sign posted on the front doors read: CLOSED UNTIL FURTHER NOTICE.

"I guess everyone was too busy to keep it running," Amy remarked.

Serena stormed past her. "I don't have time to waste!" she announced as she kicked open the doors and ran in.

Serena never thought she would ever hate being in the mall, but now she did. The Enemy had taken over *her* mall—this time it was personal!

"All right!" Amy cried as she ran behind.

"Now, we need a plan--"

"There's no time for a plan!" Serena yelled as she thrust her hand into the air. "Let's just beat these losers and get it over with! MOON PRISM POWER MAKE-UP!"

Bright lights wrapped around Serena and surrounded her with warmth. Her outfit morphed into her Sailor Moon uniform in a flurry of colors and sparkles.

"She's a little hard to keep up with," Amy said as she pulled out her transformation pen. "I'm used to Serena being lazy."

"Keep an eye on her, Amy," Luna called as she tried to keep up with them. "Serena's as impatient as when she's waiting for commercial breaks to end during *Dawson's Creek*. She's liable to make mistakes."

"Right." Amy held her pen into the air. "MERCURY POWER MAKE-UP!"

Sailor Moon hardly waited for Amy's light to disappear. They had reached the boarded-up TICKING TREASURES, and Serena wanted in. "C'mon, Amy," she insisted as she pulled her tiara from her head. "We're blasting our way through.

MOON TIARA ACTION!"

Serena flung her tiara full speed at the boarded-up door. It crashed through in a flash of golden light, opening a huge hole.

Amy raised her eyebrows. "Wow."

"Let's go," Serena called as she grabbed Amy's gloved hand and pulled her through the hole. Luna ran to follow them, but the hole suddenly sucked in behind them and turned into solid wood again.

"Ahhhh!"

Luna crashed full force into the planks. She rubbed her head painfully with her paws.

"This is terrible," she murmured breathlessly. "I can't get in there, so those girls are on their own!"

She rubbed the lump on her head and moaned. "And even worse," she muttered, "I'm turning into as bad a klutz as Serena!"

Being inside TICKING TREASURES was like being at the bottom of the ocean. It was too dark to see anything, and the air felt heavy and cold—not that there was any air at the bottom of the ocean.

Serena clenched her fists. Stupid villains, she though impatiently. She had no time for this. She had to get home—there was food to eat and games to play and TV to watch!

"So, which way do we go?" Serena asked as she looked around. "I thought super-villains usually had a lot of cash, but it looks like these ones couldn't even afford a lamp."

"They want us to get lost," Amy answered as she touched one of her earrings. A pair of transparent blue goggles lit up on her face.

Serena brightened. "Amy, when'd you get those?" she asked. "They look good on you."

Amy smiled and touched her earring again. Her goggles lit up with stats as they scanned the area. "A perk for being Sailor Mercury, I guess. They come with the suit." Amy pulled her Mercury Compact Computer out and flipped it open.

"Man, a cute little computer, too?" Serena pouted. "The only magical item I get is the Luna Pen."

"Luna tells me it's really useful," Amy said as she began to type. "You don't like it?"

"Well, I like it, but I kinda want a magic sword or something cool like that. Pens aren't really super-hero stuff, if you ask me."

Amy smiled as she closed the computer. "I think you've been reading too much *Magic Knight Rayearth*." She pointed forward. "I'm picking up readings in that direction."

"Great!" Serena shouted. They ran in the direction of the readings, and soon they saw a huge clock looming before them. It was misty, like a ghost clock, its pendulum swung menacingly.

"Welcome, Sailor Scouts." A scratchy voice hissed from the air around them.

Serena put her hands on her hips. Oh, no. These stupid bad guys weren't going to waste her time by trying to be mysterious and cunning. After all, these were the idiots who worked for that moron Jedite. Jedite, whose idea of a clever disguise was using the name JAY DIGHT.

"What are you, the ghost of Christmas Past?" Serena called impatiently. "Quit playing around and come out."

The voice roared. "Upstart! If you really want to beat me, come and find me!"

mercury rising

The pendulum in the clock disappeared, and a portal opened up in its place.

"Fine, I will."   Serena ran into the portal without a thought.

Amy blinked. "Wait!" she called as she ran after her. "Serena, don't be so impulsive!"

Inside the portal, the air was even thicker. Everything was still dark, though white doorways floated around and misty images of clocks drifted through the darkness.

"This is so lame!" Serena shouted.   "This theme of clocks and time is getting really old really fast. It's worse than the Sesame Street theme of my elementary school graduation."

"Be careful," Amy warned as she typed into her computer again.   "I have to find out which floating doorway she's hiding behind--"

"I don't have time to waste, Mercury!" Serena argued as she jumped through a doorway. "This one looks as good as any."

"No!" Amy yelled.   "Sailor Moon, not that one!"

Serena turned to look back through the doorway. "What?" she called. "This room seems the same as--hey!" Serena gasped as she began to shrink.

"What's going on?" she cried in a voice that had gone high and squeaky. "Mercury, do something!"

"Get out of that room!" Amy shouted. "This place can alter time at will. It's turning your body back into a little kid's!"

Serena suddenly remembered everything she had liked as a kid--Big Bird, sandboxes, peanut butter and jelly sandwiches...

"Ew!" she yelled as she stumbled out of the room. "I can't go back to liking that stuff, I'll be a total dork!" Then again, she thought, the peanut butter and jelly sandwiches weren't so bad.

As soon as Serena got out of the room her body grew back to normal size. She wiped her forehead in relief.

"You have to slow down and let me scan these doorways," Amy said quickly as she adjusted her goggles. "If you're not careful, another room could turn you into an old lady.

Serena gagged. That's even worse than being a kid! she thought. Then will I have to like

mercury rising

Matlock and prunes?

Amy suddenly cried out happily. "I got it," she declared as she pushed her earring and her goggles vanished. She pointed to one of the doorways to their right. "She's in there."

"Finally, we can do this!" Serena shouted as she ran through the door. She began her speech before she even saw the villain to save time.

"You've toyed with the lives of the people of this city, and that is unforgivable!" she cried, raising a fist. "I am Sailor Moon, Champion of Justice and defender of the innocent, and on behalf of the moon, you're punished!"

Amy stepped in the doorway and raised her hand. "And I'm...uh...Sailor Mercury," she announced. "I won't let you off without punishment, either."

Serena cocked an eyebrow. It looked like Amy would need some threatening-super-hero-speech training before the next battle.

The sorceress slowly floated into view, her thick hair rippling in the air. The giant misty clock faded in behind her.

"Very clever girls," she murmured in her

scratchy voice. "But you won't get any farther."

She pulled out a long wand and pointed at Serena's legs. Serena choked and fell down.

"What did you do?" she exclaimed as she tried to move. "I'm stuck!"

"I froze time for your legs, little Sailor brat," the sorceress replied with an evil chuckle. "My powers are too strong for you."

"No fair!" Serena shouted. "We don't get wands like that. You're playing dirty!"

"Ask me if I care," the villain snarled as she pointed her wand at Amy. Amy tried to dodge, but her entire body froze before she could.

"No!" Amy cried. "I can't move either!" She desperately tried to break free, but it was no use. "Sailor Moon, we have to do something!"

The sorceress laughed evilly. "No one can fight time, children." She hissed as her evil eyes flashed. "It's time to end this." She raised her wand over her head.

"You can't defeat us!" Serena yelled. "We're super-heroes! Don't you watch TV? Super-heroes always win!" Serena really hoped this lady was as stupid as Jedite, maybe she'd fall for it.

The sorceress laughed. "Well, hate to disappoint you, but this isn't TV."

"But it's a novel based on a super-hero TV show, so the rule still applies!"

The evil woman narrowed her eyes. "Shut up," she spat as she prepared to fire.

Suddenly, a rose shot out of nowhere and hit the glass of the huge ghost clock. The clock shattered into a million tiny pieces.

"No!" the sorceress yelled. "No, my precious clock!"

"Tuxedo Mask!" Serena cried happily as she felt the spell wear off. As soon as she could move her legs, she ran to find him.

"Wait, Sailor Moon!" Amy yelled as she shook her newly-freed body. "We have to beat the lady first!"

Serena scowled. Rats.

"OK, OK," she muttered as she turned back to the sorceress. "Now you'll be defeated, yadda, yadda, yadda."

Amy quickly cupped her hands. "MERCURY BUBBLES BLAST!" she shouted as she released her ball of blue light. The bubbles fogged up the room instantly, and the sorceress choked.

"I can't see!" she yelled. "You little brats, what are you doing?"

"Sending you back to the demon world or wherever the heck you stupid villains keep coming from," Serena shouted as she pulled off her tiara and threw it. "MOON TIARA ACTION!"

The sorceress screamed as the tiara shot golden light throughout her body. "NO!" she shouted. "Jedite, I will not fail you!" Her screams echoed through the air as her body vaporized, and she sprinkled slowly to the floor.

Amy clapped her hands happily. "Good work, Sailor Moon!" she cried. "You did it!"

But Serena wasn't paying attention. She was looking around, frowning sadly. "Man," she said, "Tuxedo Mask isn't here anymore. Why doesn't he ever stick around? Doesn't my beauty intrigue him?"

Amy touched her chin. "Who was that who saved us?" she asked. "I never even saw him."

Serena giggled. "Seeing him's the best part." She winked. "You could say hottie protectors are another super-hero perk. And he's much better than a magic pen."

Later on, Serena, Amy, and Luna walked down the sidewalk heading home. The city had finally calmed down to its normal state, and Serena was exhausted.

"Rushing around spent me more than I thought," she muttered as she rubbed her eyes. "I need a nap."

Amy smiled. "Well, at least you got to school on time today, Serena. How'd it feel?"

"Unnatural," Serena admitted with a grin. She suddenly remembered something, and her eyes nearly popped out of her head.

"That's right," she exclaimed, looking down at Luna. "Our bet! I made it to school on time, so you have to eat your food dish!"

Amy laughed. Luna winced.

"Uh, Serena," Luna replied, "it was just a figure of speech."

Serena laughed. "Oh, don't even try to get out of it! When we get home, you're chowing down!" She winked playfully. "Do you like salt or pepper with your plastic?"

Just then, Molly ran up. "Serena!" she cried excitedly, grabbing Serena's arm. "There's this new candy shop that just opened up. If you get there within the next five minutes, they give you a free pound!"

Serena face lit up. "Oh my God!" she shouted. "I'm there!" She grabbed Molly's hand and dashed full speed down the street.

Luna sighed as she saw Serena stumble, then trip and fall down. "That girl," she muttered as Serena began to wail, "I thought she said she was tired from all her hurrying."

Amy laughed. "If it's for candy," she answered with a wink, "Serena will do anything."

About the Writer

Lianne Sentar began her career as a writer at just 13 years-old working on an extensive fantasy novel entitled *Thief*. During the next two years, Ms. Sentar wrote hundreds of pages of fan-fiction and published them both on her website (http://members.tripod.com/~Lianne_Sentar/) as well as on other international fan-fic sites. Based on her initial online publishing success, Ms. Sentar self-published her first novella *Rain* in the fall of 1998. Since its initial release, *Rain* has been through four reprints and continues to grow in popularity. In the summer of 1999, 17-year-old Lianne began writing the *Sailor Moon* novel adaptations with the second *Sailor Moon* novel, *The Power of Love*. Ms. Sentar is currently working on her second original novel, the fantasy *Children of the Sky*. Ms. Sentar lives with her family in Connecticut, USA.